Niagara Flavours

James Lorimer & Company Ltd. acknowledges the
support of the Department of Canadian Heritage
and the Ontario Arts Council in the development
of writing and publishing in Canada.

Canadian Cataloguing in Publication Data

Matthews, Brenda
Niagara flavours
ISBN 1-55028-606-4
1. Restaurants – Ontario – Niagara Peninsula –
Guidebooks. 2. Hotels – Ontario –
Niagara Peninsula – Guidebooks. 3. Cookery –
Ontario – Niagara Peninsula. I. Title.
TX907.5.C22N52 1998   647.95713'38
C98-930216-4

James Lorimer & Company Ltd., Publishers
35 Britain Street
Toronto, Ontario
M5A 1R7

Distributed in the United States by:
Seven Hills Book Distributors
1531 Tremont Street
Cincinnati, OH 45214

Printed and bound in Canada

Acknowledgements

*I wish to thank my editor at Lorimer, Diane Young, for
her guidance and excellent suggestions. I would also like
to thank freelance editors Julia Armstrong, Jennifer
Gillard, and Eileen Koyama for their attentive copy
editing, proofreading, and eye for detail. Niagara
Flavours is an independent cookbook and guide, with no
sponsorship or fees paid for inclusion.*

*This book is dedicated to my boys: Rick, Mark, and
Christopher.*

Photo Credits
Legend: Top - T; Centre - C; Bottom - B; Right - R; Left - L
Food photography by Terry Manzo, David Smiley and Dwayne Coon. Additional photography as follows:
Dwayne Coon: p. 1; p. 8, p.17; p. 19; p. 21; p. 22; 23; 26; p. 41; p. 70; p. 72; p. 74; p. 75; p. 76; p, 80; p. 83; p. 93; p. 102; p.
109B; p.112T; p. 113B; p. 116B; p. 117B; p. 120T; p. 120C; p. 121CL; p. 121CR; p. 124CL; p. 124CR;
p. 125T; p. 126CL
Terry Manzo: p. 44; p. 94; p. 98; p. 109T; p. 116T; p. 119C; p. 122B; p. 123CL; p. 125B; p. 126CR
Jackie Noble: p. 35; p. 62; p. 66; p. 99; p. 106T; p. 110B; p. 114T; p. 115T;
David Smiley: p. 14; p. 15; p. 34; p. 36; p. 40; p. 54; p. 58; p. 61; p. 71; p. 73; p. 88; p. 95; p. 101; p. 108T; p. 108C; p. 111T;
p. 111B; p. 112B; p. 114B; p. 115B; p. 117T; p. 118; p. 119T; p. 119B; p. 121B; p. 122C; p. 123CR
Brian Thompson: p. 27; p. 110T
Willy Waterton: p. 6; p. 16; p.18; p. 31; p.32; p.33; p. 43; p. 46; p. 52; p. 53; p. 59; p. 65; p. 78; p. 84; p. 85; p. 87; p. 92; p.
104; p. 106B; p. 107T; p. 107B; p. 113T
Scott Wishart: p. 7; p.45; p.57; p.64; p.82

Niagara Flavours

Guidebook & Cookbook

BRENDA MATTHEWS

James Lorimer & Company Ltd.
Toronto 1998

CONTENTS

Flowerpot Island

INTRODUCTION

From the Niagara region in the east to Huron and Bruce Counties in the west, southwestern Ontario has the most agriculturally rich and productive farmland in the province. Blessed by the unique geography of the Niagara Escarpment and bounded by three Great Lakes, it is no wonder that this part of Ontario produces some of the best vegetables, fruit, farm-raised game, chicken, pork, beef, and fish to be found anywhere. The bountifulness of the land, in turn, has encouraged the growth of many fine inns and restaurants whose menus showcase locally grown produce and locally sourced meats.

But as wonderful as its local cuisine may be, southwestern Ontario has more to offer than just fine dining. The Niagara region, for example, has some of the most beautiful scenery in the province as well as some of the best wineries. The quality of Niagara wines has changed remarkably since the introduction of vinifera hybrids in the 1980s. Now Niagara vintages compete with some of finest in the world.

One of the best things to do in Niagara is tour the backroads, winding through orchards and vineyards from winery to winery, sipping Rieslings, Gewürztraminers, Chardonnays, and Pinot Noirs. Visitors can leisurely motor the countryside simply enjoying the view or they can sign up for tours, among them one that takes them bicycling with Canada's own Olympic medallist, Steve Bauer, who led the Tour de France on fifteen occasions. Niagara is also famous for beautiful and historic Niagara-on-the-Lake and for the Shaw Festival, running from April to October.

Huron and Bruce Counties, sharing the Lake Huron coastline, are known for miles of sandy beaches and beautiful sunsets. They are also known as the heartland of Ontario's food production. The two pretty towns of Goderich and Bayfield both have marina facilities from May to October. Fishing boats can be seen

Avon River, Stratford

leaving ports and bringing back freshly caught fish daily. Further east, the picturesque town of Stratford in Perth County is home to the famous Shakespearean Stratford Festival, running from May to November.

Niagara Flavours was written to be both a guide to the many fine establishments in this part of Ontario as well as a cookbook featuring the favourite creations of the region's best chefs. In selecting the recipes for this book, I have tried to provide a broad range for home use, covering the casual to the elegant, the simple to the challenging. As well, I have tried to maintain a balance of seafood, meat, and vegetarian dishes. The fine chefs with whom I worked in developing these recipes for home use all had something in common — a genuine pride and appreciation for their local farmers. In this part of Ontario, many chefs actually tour farms to select their produce, and it is not unusual to see local farmers profiled on menus. It is this abundance of fresh, local ingredients that makes this wonderfully creative and innovative regional cuisine.

Preparing this book was both fun and exciting. I greatly enjoyed visiting all the establishments and selecting the more than forty inns and restaurants that are included. The testing and sampling of the recipes was a gastronomic delight. I would like to thank the wonderful chefs, restaurateurs, and innkeepers for welcoming me into their kitchens and generously sharing their specialties. Each recipe reflects the quality and style of the establishment from which it came. I have included a chef's wine recommendation for each of the courses. I hope this will add to the pleasure of the experience.

Bon appetit and bon voyage!

Botanical Gardens, Niagara Peninsula

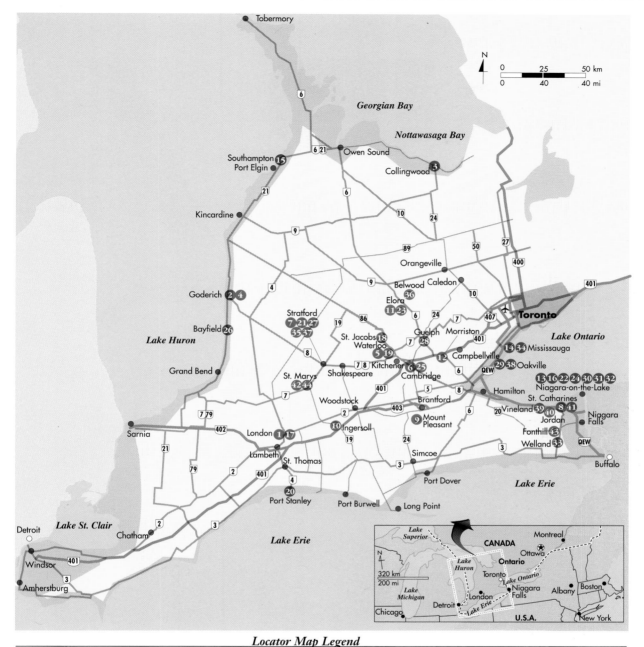

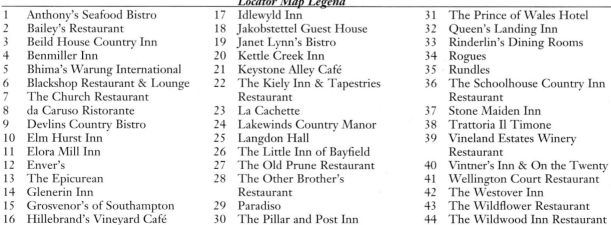

Locator Map Legend

1	Anthony's Seafood Bistro	17	Idlewyld Inn	31	The Prince of Wales Hotel
2	Bailey's Restaurant	18	Jakobstettel Guest House	32	Queen's Landing Inn
3	Beild House Country Inn	19	Janet Lynn's Bistro	33	Rinderlin's Dining Rooms
4	Benmiller Inn	20	Kettle Creek Inn	34	Rogues
5	Bhima's Warung International	21	Keystone Alley Café	35	Rundles
6	Blackshop Restaurant & Lounge	22	The Kiely Inn & Tapestries	36	The Schoolhouse Country Inn
7	The Church Restaurant		Restaurant		Restaurant
8	da Caruso Ristorante	23	La Cachette	37	Stone Maiden Inn
9	Devlins Country Bistro	24	Lakewinds Country Manor	38	Trattoria Il Timone
10	Elm Hurst Inn	25	Langdon Hall	39	Vineland Estates Winery
11	Elora Mill Inn	26	The Little Inn of Bayfield		Restaurant
12	Enver's	27	The Old Prune Restaurant	40	Vintner's Inn & On the Twenty
13	The Epicurean	28	The Other Brother's	41	Wellington Court Restaurant
14	Glenerin Inn		Restaurant	42	The Westover Inn
15	Grosvenor's of Southampton	29	Paradiso	43	The Wildflower Restaurant
16	Hillebrand's Vineyard Café	30	The Pillar and Post Inn	44	The Wildwood Inn Restaurant

Quail Mousseline with Balsamic Carmelized Onions and Cheese Crisps

APPETIZERS

An appetizer is the first thing that guests taste when they come to your home. The first course is important because it sets the mood and whets the tastebuds for the courses that follow.

Some of the recipes included here are "finger foods," easily eaten while standing — perfect for a cocktail party. Others require a plate and fork and are more elegant appetizers, best suited as sit-down openers to a formal dinner.

This section offers a variety of delicious recipes. Some are very quick and easy to prepare like Crab Dip and Carrot Dip from the Beild House Country Inn and Smoked Trout Rillette from the Old Prune Restaurant. Others — Goat Cheese Soufflé with Lettuces and Marinated Vegetables from The Church Restaurant or Quail Mousseline with Balsamic Caramelized Onions and Cheese Crisps from Hillebrand's Vineyard Cafe — are more challenging but well worth the effort. Enjoy the exotic flavours of Thai Shrimp from Bailey's, Mussels Steamed in Thai Citrus and Coconut Broth from Wellington Court or Cha Gio from Bhima's Warung International. Many of these recipes can easily be served as a light dinner or luncheon dish by increasing the serving portion.

Mussels Steamed in Thai Citrus and Coconut Broth

MUSSELS STEAMED IN THAI CITRUS AND COCONUT BROTH
Wellington Court
Executive Chef: Erik Peacock

These steamed mussels feature wonderful Thai flavours. Serve with a soup spoon to be sure to consume the unbelievably good broth. Chef Peacock advises keeping the mussels refrigerated until just before cooking.

3 lb mussels (about 75)
2 tbsp butter
1/2 small onion, minced
1 clove garlic, minced
1 tsp minced lemongrass
1/4 tsp minced fresh gingerroot
1 can (14 fl. oz) coconut milk
2 tbsp granulated sugar
1 tsp chili paste
juice of 1 lime
juice of 1 lemon
juice of 2 oranges
2 tbsp chopped fresh cilantro

Scrub and debeard mussels. Discard any that do not close when tapped.

Melt butter in a large saucepan over medium-high heat. Sauté onion, garlic, lemongrass and ginger for about 3 minutes. Add coconut milk, sugar, chili paste and lime, lemon and orange juices. Bring to simmer; add mussels and steam, stirring once, until they open. (Discard any that have not opened.) Divide broth and mussels among 6 shallow bowls; sprinkle with cilantro. Serves 6 as a first course.

Chef's wine suggestion — Gewürztraminer, Château des Charmes

THAI SHRIMP
Bailey's
Owner/Chef: Ben Merritt

Serve these beautiful, piquant shrimp with a simple mixed green salad or cold noodle salad.

36 large shrimp, peeled and deveined (tail intact)

Marinade
1/2 cup lemon juice
1/4 cup smooth peanut butter
1/4 cup fresh minced gingerroot
1 tbsp olive oil
1 tsp brown sugar
1 tsp Tabasco Sauce
1 tsp curry paste (preferably Hot Patak's)
2 cloves garlic
1/4 tsp salt
1/4 tsp pepper

In food processor or blender, combine lemon juice, peanut butter, gingerroot, oil, brown sugar, Tabasco Sauce, curry paste, garlic, salt and pepper; blend thoroughly. In glass or ceramic bowl, combine shrimp with marinade; let stand for 10 minutes.

Transfer shrimp to barbecue grill over medium heat; grill until just opaque. Serves 6 as a first course.

Chef's wine suggestion — Gewürztraminer, VQA, 1996, Vineland Estates

SMOKED TROUT RILLETTE
The Old Prune Restaurant
Sous-Chef: Deborah Reid

This makes deliciously simple appetizers or hors d' oeuvres. It can be prepared in advance and refrigerated for up to four days.

2 whole smoked trout, each 1 1/2 lb
2 shallots, finely chopped
1/4 cup finely chopped mixed herbs (tarragon, chives and parsley)
3/4 cup mayonnaise
lemon juice
salt and pepper

Fillet the trout, discarding skin, head and bones. Remove fine pin bones that run the length of the fillets. Roughly crumble fillets into bowl. Add shallots, herbs and mayonnaise; stir together. Add lemon juice and salt and pepper to taste.

Divide among individual 1/2-cup ramekins or small bowls. For appetizer or light lunch: Serve with green salad and baguette. For hors d'oeuvres: Spread on small toasts or sliced cucumber rounds. Makes 4 appetizer servings, each 1/2 cup.

Chef's wine suggestion — Riesling Reserve, 1995, Cave Spring Cellars

Stratford countryside

George Park, Elora

MOULES À LA PROVENÇALE (PROVENÇAL MUSSELS)

La Cachette
Owner/Chef: Alain Levesque

Serve this delicious classic mussel dish with some crusty bread to soak up the juices in the bowl. Garnish with chopped roasted peppers or tomato if desired.

4 1/2 lb mussels
1 1/2 cups dry white wine
6 tbsp chopped onions
4 tbsp butter
1/4 cup chopped mixed fresh herbs (thyme, rosemary and oregano) or 2 tbsp dried
2 tbsp finely chopped shallots
2 tbsp minced garlic
2 tbsp finely chopped fresh parsley
4 bay leaves
pinch crushed black peppercorns
pinch salt
2 medium tomatoes, chopped

Scrub and debeard mussels. Discard any that do not open when tapped. In large pot over high heat, combine mussels, wine, onions, butter, herbs, shallots, garlic, parsley, bay leaves, peppercorns and salt. Cover and bring to boil. Boil for 5 minutes or until mussels open. Gently shake several times to distribute ingredients and release flavour. Discard bay leaves and any mussels that do not open. Garnish with tomatoes. Serve in soup bowls with inverted soup bowls on top to act as lids to keep warm; use empty bowls for discarding shells. Serves 6 as a first course.

Chef's wine suggestion — Pinot Grigio, VQA, 1996, Inniskillin

BLACKSHOP MARINATED SALMON
Blackshop Restaurant & Lounge
Executive Chefs: Alex Vetrovsky & Ladislav Kilian

The longer this succulent salmon is marinated, the more predominant the dill, pepper and Pernod flavours will be. The chefs at Blackshop recommend that an ideal marination time is 18 hours, but personal preference will determine yours.

3/4 cup granulated sugar
1 cup lemon juice
1/4 cup Pernod
3 tbsp salt
1 fresh salmon fillet (skin on), 3 lb
1/2 bunch fresh dill, chopped
3 tbsp crushed black peppercorns
2 lemons, cut into wedges
1 small bottle (4.4 oz) capers
1 red onion, sliced

Sauce
1/2 cup coarse Pommery (or grainy old-fashioned) mustard
1 tbsp chopped fresh dill
1 tbsp brown sugar

In glass or porcelain container with edges high enough to be able to fully submerge fish in marinade, combine sugar, lemon juice, Pernod and salt.

Place fish on work surface, skin side down. Spoon marinade over skinless side. Cover with dill and peppercorns. Place skinless side down in marinade; cover tightly and let marinate in refrigerator for at least 12 hours or for up to 36 hours, turning occasionally.

Sauce: Combine mustard, dill and sugar, stirring until sugar is dissolved.

To serve, slice salmon into paper-thin slices using sharp filleting knife. Fan slices on each of 10 chilled plates. Garnish with lemon wedge, capers, onion slices and sauce. Serves 10.

Chef's wine suggestion — Gewürztraminer, Henry of Pelham

CRAB DIP
Beild House Country Inn
Owner/Chef: Bill Barclay

This delicious dip is another favourite at the inn. Serve hot with crackers.

8 oz cream cheese
1 can (4 oz) crab meat or sea legs
1 tbsp mayonnaise
2 tsp horseradish
1 tsp curry powder
1 dash Worcestershire sauce

Combine cream cheese, crab meat, mayonnaise, horseradish, curry powder and Worcestershire sauce; mix well. Pour into shell or small baking dish. Bake in 250°F oven for about 30 minutes or until golden and bubbly. Makes about 1 1/2 cups.

Chef's wine suggestion — Trius, Brut, Hillebrand Estates

Blackshop Restaurant and Lounge, Cambridge

CHA GIO
Bhima's Warung International
Owner/Chef: Paul Boehmer

Chef Boehmer says that this is one of Vietnam's most famous national dishes. These rice paper rounds can be stuffed with just about anything you like. They make excellent cocktail hors d'oeuvres. Cha gio is traditionally served with nuoc cham *dipping sauce (see recipe below).*

1 cup glass noodles
1 lb lean ground pork
1 cup salad crab
2 eggs
1/4 cup fish sauce (preferably nam pla or nuoc nam)
1 tbsp chopped fresh mint
1 tbsp chopped fresh cilantro
1 tbsp chopped Thai basil
1 tsp pepper
20 rice paper wrappers (6 inches in diameter)
2 tbsp vegetable oil

Soak noodles in warm water for about 10 minutes or until soft. Cut into 1-inch lengths.

In bowl, mix together pork, crab, eggs, fish sauce, mint, cilantro, basil and pepper. Working with 2 or 3 rice paper wrappers at a time, soak in warm water until pliable, about 1 minute. (Don't leave them too long or they will tear.)

Lay soaked wrappers on surface; spoon about 1/2 tbsp of the pork mixture just below centre. Fold over sides and roll up into cylinder. Place, seam side down, on baking sheet and cover with towel to prevent drying out. Repeat with remaining wrappers and pork mixture.

In ovenproof skillet, heat oil over medium-high heat; fry cha gio, turning occasionally until browned all over. Transfer to baking sheet and cook in 400°F oven for 10 minutes longer. Makes 20 rice paper rounds.

Nuoc Cham
2 tbsp granulated sugar
1/2 cup warm water
1 cup nuoc nam (fish sauce)
2 tbsp lime juice
1 tbsp vinegar
1/2 tsp minced garlic
1/2 tsp chopped Thai (bird) chilies

Dissolve sugar in warm water; stir in nuoc nam, lime juice, vinegar, garlic and chilies. Serve with cha gio.

Chef's wine suggestion — Dry Riesling, Cave Spring Cellars

Queen's Valley, Georgian Bay Country

JOE SPECK FARMS QUAIL MOUSSELINE WITH BALSAMIC CARAMELIZED ONIONS AND CHEESE CRISPS
Hillebrand's Vineyard Café
Executive Chef: Tony de Luca

Chef de Luca recommends this appetizer as an ideal introduction to quail because it combines quail and chicken meat. The mousseline is very smooth and delicate. Joe Speck is a local Niagara quail farmer.

3 oz boneless chicken breast
6 oz boneless quail breast
1 tbsp butter
1 tbsp olive oil
1 leek (white part only), finely diced
5 large shiitake mushrooms (stems removed), finely diced
2 medium shallots, finely diced
1 1/2 cups 35% cream
3 1/4 cups strong chicken stock
salt and pepper

Remove skin and all sinew from chicken and quail. In skillet, heat butter and oil over medium heat; sauté leeks, mushrooms and shallots for 3 minutes. Remove from heat and refrigerate until chilled.

In food processor, purée chicken and quail until smooth. Using a pastry spatula, pass the purée through a fine strainer or sieve. Refrigerate until chilled thoroughly. Blend cream into purée. Stir in leek mixture and 1/4 cup of the stock. Season with salt and pepper to taste. Refrigerate until chilled.

Using 2 tablespoons, form quenelles from quail mousseline (See chef's tip). Bring remaining stock to boil; reduce heat and simmer. Plunge quenelles into stock; cook for about 4 minutes or until firm to the touch.

Chef's tip: To shape quenelles, set 1 metal tablespoon in bowl of hot water. Using another tablespoon, scoop out enough of the quail mousseline to fill it. Invert hot, moist spoon over filled spoon. Smoothing surface but without pressing hard, form into egg shape. After shaping, invert onto greased surface. Repeat with remaining mixture.

Caramelized Onions
1 tsp unsalted butter
1 tsp extra-virgin olive oil
1 medium onion, julienned
2 tbsp balsamic vinegar
1 tsp finely chopped lemon thyme
salt and pepper

In small saucepan, melt butter over medium-low heat. Add oil when butter foams. Add onions and cook, stirring constantly, until glossy brown. Remove from heat. Stir in balsamic vinegar and lemon thyme. Let stand until mixture comes to room temperature.

Cheese Crisps
1/2 cup freshly grated Montasio, Asiago or Parmesan cheese

On nonstick baking sheet, spoon 1 tbsp of the cheese into mound. Repeat to make 7 more mounds. Bake in 350°F oven just until golden brown. Remove from oven and let cool to room temperature.

To Assemble: Place 2 cheese crisps on each of the 4 warmed plates. Spoon caramelized onions over cheese crisps. Top each with quail mousseline. Serves 4 as a first course.

Chef's wine suggestion — Trius, Brut, Hillebrand Estates

Beaver Valley

SMOKED CHICKEN SPRING ROLLS
The Schoolhouse Country Inn Restaurant
Owner/Chef: Peter Egger

Wonderfully fresh and full of flavour, these are ideal for a cocktail party.

1 cup thinly sliced Napa cabbage
3/4 cup cooked rice
1/3 cup julienned smoked chicken
2 green onions, chopped
1 clove garlic, minced
1 1/2 tbsp soy sauce
1/2 tbsp fish sauce
1/2 tbsp toasted sesame seeds
1 tsp chopped fresh cilantro
1 tsp Tabasco Sauce
1 tsp sesame oil
1/2 tsp grated fresh gingerroot
10 rice paper wrappers (6 inches in diameter)

Steam cabbage very briefly. Stir together cabbage, rice, chicken, onions, garlic, soy sauce, fish sauce, sesame seeds, cilantro, Tabasco Sauce, sesame oil and ginger.

Working with 1 or 2 wrappers at a time and keeping remaining covered to prevent drying out, brush with water to moisten and place on clean cloth. Spoon filling in centre of wrapper; fold over edges and roll up to completely enclose filling. Repeat with remaining wrappers and filling. Wrap securely in plastic wrap and refrigerate until serving. Makes 10 rolls.

Chef's wine suggestion — Auxerros, Inniskillin

The Epicurean, Niagara-on-the-Lake

CLOVER HONEY ROASTED QUAIL WITH PEACH GRAVY ON RUBY CHARD
The Pillar and Post Inn
Executive Chef: Virginia Marr

Chef Marr says that this delectable appetizer recipe would also work well with pheasant. Use two pheasants and cut them in half just before serving.

Peach Gravy
4 peaches, pitted, peeled and diced
2 tbsp brown sugar
3 tbsp all-purpose flour
3 cups hot chicken broth
1 sweet green pepper, seeded and diced

In saucepan over medium heat, cook peaches with brown sugar, stirring occasionally, until caramelized. Add flour and cook for 3 to 5 minutes, stirring with wooden spoon to scrape up brown bits from bottom of pan and prevent sticking. Pour in hot chicken broth 1/2 cup at a time. Add green pepper. Cook for 15 to 20 minutes or until flour is cooked out. Strain through fine sieve into another saucepan. If necessary, reduce again to achieve desired consistency.

Rice Mixture
1 cup wild rice, cooked and chilled
4 large tiger shrimp, peeled, deveined and coarsely chopped
1 roasted red pepper, peeled, seeded and diced
1 clove garlic, minced
2 shallots, minced
2 tbsp melted unsalted butter
salt and pepper

In bowl, combine rice, shrimp, roasted peppers, garlic, shallots, butter and salt and pepper to taste. Set aside.

Quails
3 tbsp clover honey
2 tbsp aged balsamic vinegar
salt and pepper
4 large deboned quails
4 strips European bacon*
1 bunch chard
2 tbsp herb oil
2 tbsp chopped fresh chives

In bowl, blend together honey, balsamic vinegar and salt and pepper to taste. Spread quails open and fill with rice mixture. Fold back together and wrap with bacon strips. Secure with skewer or toothpick. Glaze quails modestly with honey mixture. Roast in 375°F oven, glazing frequently, for 15 to 20 minutes or until golden brown.

To Assemble: Tear chard into bite-size pieces and toss with herb oil. Mound on each of 4 plates. Place quail on top and coat with peach gravy. Garnish with chives. Serves 4 as a first course.

* European bacon is a double smoked fresh bacon.

Chef's wine suggestion — Cabernet Merlot, 1995, Cave Spring Cellars

WARM SMOKED DUCK SALAD
The Epicurean Fine Foods
Owner/Chef: Ruth Aspinall

This recipe also works very well with boneless skinless chicken breasts sautéed or grilled until no longer pink inside. A robust bread such as focaccia or herb bread goes well with the salad. It will serve eight as an appetizer or four as a main course. Chef Aspinall suggests serving the salsa over grilled fish, too.

Citrus Salsa Dressing
1/3 cup finely chopped onion
1/2 cup lemon juice
3 tbsp grated orange rind
3/4 cup orange juice
1/2 tsp salt
1/4 tsp pepper
1 cup virgin olive oil

In food processor or in bowl using whisk, combine onion, lemon juice, orange rind, orange juice, salt and pepper. With motor running, gradually pour in oil. (Can be stored in refrigerator for up to 1 day.)

2 tomatoes, seeded and chopped
1/2 cup chopped fresh mint
1/2 cup chopped fresh basil
1/2 cup chopped fresh cilantro
4 smoked duck breasts
mesclun or mixed salad greens to serve 8

Combine tomatoes, mint, basil and cilantro; toss with dressing. Marinate for 1 hour.

In skillet, sauté smoked duck breasts until heated through and fat is rendered out of skin.

Arrange greens on 8 plates. Slice duck and arrange on greens. Drizzle with citrus salsa dressing. Serves 8.

Chef's wine suggestion — Gewürztraminer, VQA, 1996, Vineland Estates

DUCK CRÊPES
Elora Mill Country Inn
Executive Chef: Randy Landry

This is a very elegant appetizer. It's rich with wonderful flavours.

Crêpes
1 lb duck meat
1/4 cup sherry
pinch each chopped fresh basil and thyme
salt and pepper
3 tbsp apple chutney
phyllo pastry
1/4 cup vegetable oil
10 oz (approx) Brie cheese

Sauce
1/4 cup 35% cream
1/4 cup apple cider
1/4 cup Calvados
salt and pepper

Cut duck into 1- x 1/2-inch strips. Combine sherry, basil, thyme and salt and pepper to taste. Add duck strips, turning to coat; marinate for about 30 minutes.

In saucepan over medium heat, sauté duck and sherry marinade for 5 minutes or until

cooked through. Reduce heat to low and add chutney; cook for 10 minutes. Season with salt and pepper to taste. Let cool.

Sauce: In separate saucepan over medium-high heat, stir cream with cider and reduce by half. Add Calvados and reduce a little more. Season with salt and pepper to taste. Remove from heat.

Layer 3 sheets of phyllo pastry on top of one another. Cut to width of 2 inches. Brush with oil and top with one-tenth of the duck mixture. Cut Brie into strips and place on top. Roll up and place on baking sheet. Repeat with remaining phyllo, oil, duck mixture and Brie.

Brush crêpes with oil; bake in 350°F oven for 10 to 15 minutes or until golden brown. Place 2 crêpes on each plate. Gently heat sauce and spoon over top. Makes 10 crêpes. Serves 5 as a first course (2 crêpes each).

Chef's wine suggestion — Chardonnay, Cave Spring Cellars

Niagara-on-the-Lake

MINI PANCAKES (POFFERTJES) WITH LAMB CROQUETTES AND BLUEBERRY CHUTNEY

Vineland Estates Winery Restaurant
Executive Chef: Mark Picone

Poffertjes are a traditional Dutch treat, available from street vendors on market day. This version is not the traditional sweet one, but rather savoury.

Blueberry Chutney
2 cups blueberries
1 cup Riesling wine
1/3 cup granulated sugar
1 cinnamon stick

In saucepan over medium heat, combine blueberries, wine, sugar and cinnamon stick; cook until reduced by half. Remove cinnamon stick. Let cool.

Lamb Croquettes
3/4 lb ground lamb
1/4 cup bread crumbs
3 tbsp coarsely chopped pistachios
2 tbsp coarsely chopped dried cherries
1 egg
salt and pepper

In bowl, combine lamb, bread crumbs, pistachios, cherries, egg and salt and pepper to taste; mix thoroughly. Shape into 2-inch patties (about 3/4 inch thick) and place on baking sheet. Bake in 200°F oven for about 20 minutes. Set aside.

Mini Pancakes
3/4 cup all-purpose flour
1 tbsp baking powder
1 tsp granulated sugar
1 tsp salt
pepper
1/3 cup milk
2 tbsp sour cream
2 tbsp olive oil
1 egg
1 tbsp finely chopped fresh rosemary

In bowl, combine flour, baking powder, sugar, salt and pepper to taste. Add milk, sour cream, oil, egg and rosemary. Stir until well combined.

Heat greased nonstick skillet over medium-low heat; using about 1 tbsp per pancake, drop batter into skillet. Cook until underside is golden brown. Turn and cook until other side is golden brown. Keep warm in oven.

Place 2 or 3 pancakes on each of 6 plates. Top with lamb croquette and blueberry chutney. Serves 6 as a first course.

Chef's wine suggestion — Cabernet-Franc Rose, 1996, Vineland Estates

TOMATO BASIL TART

On The Twenty Restaurant & Wine Bar
Vintner's Inn
Executive Chef: Michael Olson

Chef Olson says that this tart is the living end when the tomatoes are fresh from the field.

Pastry

1 cup all-purpose flour
1/2 tsp salt
1/2 cup cold unsalted butter
ice water

Combine flour with salt; cut in butter until mixture resembles coarse meal. Gradually pour in ice water until dough forms ball. Wrap in plastic wrap and refrigerate for 1 hour.

Roll out pastry and line 9-inch French tart pan or pie plate. Cover with foil and line with pie weights. Bake in 350°F oven for 12 minutes. Remove weights and foil.

Filling

3 to 4 medium tomatoes, cut into wedges (or 2 pints cherry tomatoes, cut in half)
1/2 cup grated Romano cheese
2 tbsp extra-virgin olive oil
2 tbsp chopped fresh basil
1 tsp chopped fresh thyme
1 clove garlic, minced
salt and pepper

Increase oven temperature to 400°F. In bowl, toss together tomatoes, cheese, oil, basil, thyme, garlic and salt and pepper to taste. Spoon into pastry shell and bake for 7 to 9 minutes or just until cheese starts to brown. (Do not overbake, as tomato juices will soften crust.) Serves 4 to 6 as a first course.

Chef's tip: If you don't have pie weights, rice or dried beans work just as well.

Chef's wine suggestion — Gamay, Cave Spring Cellars

Niagara Falls

Goat Cheese Soufflé

GOAT CHEESE SOUFFLÉ WITH LETTUCES AND MARINATED VEGETABLES

The Church Restaurant
Owner/Chef: Sheldon Russell

This great-tasting soufflé is an embellishment of the basic cheese soufflé. It captures the smells and tastes of the Mediterranean.

Soufflé

1 tomato
2 tbsp freshly grated Parmesan cheese
2 tbsp bread crumbs
1 1/8 cup milk
3/4 cup 35% cream
3 tbsp butter + 1 tsp
1/3 cup all-purpose flour + 1 tsp
3 egg yolks
8 oz goat cheese (chèvre)
1/2 tsp chopped fresh thyme
1/2 tsp chopped fresh oregano
5 egg whites
6 kalamata olives, pitted and diced
1 tsp lemon rind, blanched and chopped

Blanch tomato in boiling water; skin, seed and dice. Set aside. Butter ramekins. Combine Parmesan cheese with bread crumbs; line ramekins with mixture, shaking off any excess.

In saucepan, bring milk and cream to boil. Remove from heat. In separate saucepan over medium heat, melt all of the butter. Gradually add the flour and cook, stirring constantly, for about 3 minutes. Gradually add milk mixture, stirring constantly to prevent lumps. Bring to boil and reduce heat to low and simmer, stirring constantly, for 1 minute. Remove from heat.

In large bowl, cream yolks with 6 oz of the goat cheese. Blend in thyme and oregano. Gradually pour milk mixture over goat cheese mixture, whisking until thoroughly incorporated.

Beat egg whites until stiff, smooth peaks form; mix one-quarter into soufflé mixture. Fold in remaining egg whites.

Spoon into ramekins, filling about halfway. Sprinkle with some of the olives, tomatoes and lemon rind. Spoon in remaining soufflé mixture, filling almost to top. Sprinkle with remaining olives, tomatoes and lemon rind.

Crumble remaining goat cheese into pea-size pieces; sprinkle on top.

Pour enough hot water into roasting pan to come 1/2 inch up sides. Place the ramekins in pan and bake in 350°F oven for 10 to 15 minutes. Let cool for 15 minutes. Shaking ramekins gently from side to side, invert onto nonstick baking sheet or sheet lined with parchment or waxed paper. (Can be refrigerated for up to 1 day.)

Salad

1/3 cup virgin olive oil
4 tsp hazelnut oil
2 tbsp white or red wine vinegar
1/2 small red onion, julienned
1/4 each sweet red and yellow pepper, julienned
1 small zucchini, julienned
1 small carrot, julienned
mesclun or mixed lettuces to serve 6
salt and pepper

Whisk together olive oil, hazelnut oil and vinegar. In nonstick skillet, heat 2 tbsp of the vinaigrette over medium heat; sauté onion, red and yellow peppers, zucchini and carrot until limp but still crisp. Let cool; add to remaining vinaigrette and salt and pepper to taste. (Can be refrigerated for up to 1 day.)

To Assemble: Place soufflés on cookie sheet and heat in 375°F oven for about 10 minutes or until puffed.

Meanwhile, strain vinaigrette from vegetables, reserving vinaigrette. Toss vinaigrette with mesclun. Arrange vegetables in centre of each of 6 plates. Arrange mesclun around vegetables. Top with soufflé. Serves 6.

Chef's wine suggestion — Gewürztraminer, Cave Spring Cellars

Stuffed Portobello Mushrooms

STUFFED PORTOBELLO MUSHROOMS ON MIXED GREENS
The Prince of Wales Hotel
Executive Chef: Ralf Bretzigheimer

The mushrooms and vinaigrette can be prepared a day or two before serving this mouth-watering appetizer.

Vinaigrette
1/2 cup vegetable oil
1/3 cup maple syrup
2 tbsp balsamic vinegar
2 tbsp white vinegar
salt and pepper

In food processor or blender, mix together oil, maple syrup, balsamic vinegar, white vinegar and salt and pepper to taste until creamy. (You can also use a jar with a tight-fitting lid and shake vigorously.)

Salad
6 medium portobello mushrooms
1/4 cup olive oil
1 white onion, thinly sliced
2 tbsp port
salt and pepper
1 package fresh spinach, washed, dried and steamed
3 oz Woolwich goat cheese, sliced into 6 pieces
mesclun or mixed greens to serve 6
1/4 cup diced sweet red pepper
1/4 cup diced sweet yellow pepper

Remove stems from mushrooms and wipe caps with wet cloth.

In skillet, heat 2 tbsp of the oil over medium heat; sauté onions until caramelized and light brown. Add port and salt and pepper to taste. Set aside on small plate.

In clean skillet, briefly sauté spinach in 1 tbsp of the remaining oil until wilted; transfer to plate. Sauté mushrooms in remaining tablespoon of oil until soft.

Place mushroom caps on small baking sheet. Fill caps with caramelized onions, then 1 slice of goat cheese. Top with spinach.

Bake in 350°F oven for 5 to 8 minutes or until cheese is melted.

Meanwhile, arrange mesclun on each of 6 plates; sprinkle with diced peppers. Place heated mushrooms in centre of greens. Drizzle with vinaigrette. Serves 6.

Chef's wine suggestion — Chardonnay, Inniskillin

CUCUMBER GOAT CHEESE TORTE
On The Twenty Restaurant & Wine Bar
Vintner's Inn
Executive Chef: Michael Olson

Chef Olson suggests serving this fresh and creamy torte with sliced hothouse tomatoes drizzled with fine-quality extra-virgin olive oil.

Devlin's Bistro, Mount Pleasant

1 English cucumber, sliced
salt and pepper
8 oz goat cheese (chèvre)
1 tsp chopped fresh basil
1 tsp chopped fresh mint
1 tsp chopped fresh chives
1/4 to 1/3 cup 35% cream

Slice cucumber thinly. Sprinkle with a little salt. Let drain in colander.

In bowl, blend together cheese, basil, mint, chives and salt and pepper to taste. Gradually stir in enough cream to soften until spreadable but not too thin.

Line bottoms and sides of 4 6-oz ramekins with cucumber slices, overlapping slightly. Divide filling equally among ramekins. Top with layer of cucumber. Refrigerate for at least 1 hour or overnight.

To serve, gently run knife along edge of ramekins and turn out onto plates. Serves 4 as a first course.

Chef's wine suggestion — Off Dry Riesling, Cave Spring Cellars

ARTICHOKE STRUDEL
Devlin's Country Bistro
Owner/Chef: Chris Devlin

This tasty strudel can be served in large pieces for an appetizer or cut into small pieces and served as hors d'oeuvres. It can be prepared a day ahead and baked just before serving.

1 pkg (16 oz) phyllo pastry
melted unsalted butter
1 can (14 oz) artichoke hearts, drained well, sliced
10 oz (approx) shredded Asiago cheese
pepper
oil-packed sun-dried tomatoes, drained, chopped

Lay 1 sheet of phyllo pastry on work surface and brush lightly with melted butter. Fold in half. Repeat with second sheet of phyllo and lay on top of first. Place a few sliced artichoke hearts in centre; sprinkle with Asiago cheese, pepper and a few sun-dried tomato pieces. Fold edges over, tucking all ingredients under phyllo. Roll up tightly without tearing dough. Place on baking sheet. Brush lightly with butter. Repeat to make as many rolls as desired.

Bake in 425°F oven for about 12 minutes or until golden brown. Makes 10 large strudels.

Chef's wine suggestion — Riesling Dry, Vineland Estates

CARROT DIP
Beild House Country Inn
Owner/Chef: Bill Barclay

This dip is the most popular hors d'oeuvre at Beild House, where it is always served as part of predinner goodies. Serve with crackers.

1/2 cup shredded peeled carrots
1/2 cup freshly grated Parmesan cheese
1/4 cup mayonnaise

Stir together carrots, Parmesan cheese and mayonnaise and pour into shell or small baking dish. Bake in 225°F oven for about 30 minutes or until puffy and golden. Makes about 1 cup.

Chef's tip: Avoid a hotter oven or else the mayonnaise may separate and the dish can become greasy.

Chef's wine suggestion — Trius, Brut, Hillebrand Estates

Mussel Chowder with Root Vegetables and Fresh Dill

SOUPS

A pot of hearty soup simmering on the stove has an irresistible appeal. Filling the house with tantalizing aromas, soup is the perfect way to warm the soul on a cold and blustery day.

Served as a first course, it is an elegant and cosy way to begin a dinner party. Accompanied with a crusty loaf and salad, it makes a delicious and nourishing lunch or light dinner. And, of course, a cold soup is a lovely way to begin a summer meal.

Enjoy the bounty of the sea with Soup Provençal from Anthony's Seafood Bistro, Oriental Bouillabaisse from the Kiely Inn and Tapestries Restaurant or Mussel Chowder with Root Vegetables and Fresh Dill from the Westover Inn. Or refresh the palate on a warm summer day with Niagara Gazpacho from Wellington Court.

At least one or two recipes from this collection of great soups are bound to become favourites!

ORIENTAL BOUILLABAISSE

The Kiely Inn & Tapestries Restaurant
Executive Chef: Vincent Sica

Finishing with the gin and spices in this recipe adds an extra bite and unique flavour. You can make it as mild or spicy as you wish.

1/4 cup butter
1/2 cup diced carrots
1/2 cup diced celery
1 large onion, diced
2 bay leaves
1 tbsp finely chopped fresh tarragon
1 tbsp finely chopped fresh oregano
salt and pepper
4 cups puréed tomatoes
6 cups homemade fish stock or fish bouillon
1 lb mussels
8 to 10 shrimp, peeled and deveined (tail intact)
1 white fish fillet (sole, bass, cod, flounder, etc.), 8 oz
1/2 cup gin
2 tbsp lemon juice
dash Tabasco Sauce
dash Worcestershire sauce
1/4 cup chopped fresh parsley

In skillet, heat butter over medium heat; sauté carrots, celery and onions for about 8 minutes or until tender. Add bay leaves, tarragon, oregano and salt and pepper to taste; cook for 3 minutes. Mix in puréed tomatoes and fish stock; cook for 5 minutes longer. Remove bay leaves. Purée mixture in batches in food processor or blender.

Return to pot. Bring to boil and simmer for 15 to 20 minutes. Scrub and debeard mussels. Discard any that do not open when tapped. Add mussels, shrimp and fish during last 10 minutes of cooking. Add gin, lemon juice, Tabasco Sauce and Worcestershire sauce. Taste and adjust salt and pepper to taste if necessary. (Discard any mussels that have not opened.) Ladle into bowls and garnish with parsley. Serves 8 as a first course.

Chef's wine suggestion — Riesling Reserve, 1995, Henry of Pelham

Oriental Bouillabaisse

Soup Provençal
Anthony's
Owner/Chef: David Chapman

This superb-tasting soup is full of flavour and easy to prepare. It's a wonderful way to enjoy fish. If you don't have time to make your own fish stock, Knorr Instant Seafood Stock Mix or chicken stock works well.

Rouille
1 cup mayonnaise
1/4 cup pimientos, drained
3 small cloves garlic, minced
dash Pernod (optional)

In food processor or blender, combine mayonnaise, pimientos, garlic and Pernod (if using): blend until smooth. Set aside.

Soup
12 mussels
8 large tiger shrimp
8 large sea scallops
1 lb firm fish (swordfish, halibut, or monkfish)
1 medium leek (white and light green part only)
1 large Yukon Gold potato (unpeeled)
1 tbsp olive oil
4 cups homemade fish stock
2 cloves garlic, minced
pinch saffron
2 medium tomatoes, coarsely chopped
1 baguette

Scrub mussels and remove beards. Discard any that do not close when tapped. Clean shrimp, scallops and fish under cold running water and pat dry with paper towels. Peel and devein shrimp. Cut scallops in half. Cut fish into 1 1/2-inch pieces.

Thoroughly wash leek under cold running water; slice coarsely. Scrub potato; cut into quarters, then cut into 1/4-inch-thick slices. In large saucepan, heat oil over medium heat; sauté leeks until soft. Add stock, potato slices, garlic and saffron; bring to boil and simmer until potatoes are al dente.

Add mussels, shrimp, scallops, fish and tomatoes; simmer for about 3 minutes or until seafood is opaque. Discard any mussels that have not opened.

Slice 6 1/2-inch-thick pieces of baguette; toast under broiler until golden. Lay 1 slice in bottom of each of 6 soup bowls; spoon dollop of rouille on top of toast and ladle soup over top. Serves 6 as a first course.

Chef's wine suggestion — Gewürztraminer, Pelee Island

Tobermory

MUSSEL CHOWDER WITH ROOT VEGETABLES AND FRESH DILL

The Westover Inn
Executive Chef: Michael Hoy

This is a deliciously rich, full-flavoured chowder that can also be enjoyed for lunch with a crusty loaf of bread. If you don't have time to make a fresh fish stock, Knorr makes a good instant seafood stock mix.

Fish Stock

1 tsp unsalted butter
1 lb halibut bones or any white fish bones
3 1/2 cups cold water
1 small onion, chopped
1 stalk celery, chopped
1 bay leaf
6 whole black peppercorns
sprig each fresh thyme and parsley (or 1/4 tsp each dried)
salt and pepper

Chop fish bones about 3 inches long.

In skillet, melt butter over very low heat; sauté fish bones, covered, for 10 minutes. Add cold water, onion, celery, bay leaf, peppercorns, thyme, parsley and salt and pepper to taste. Simmer, uncovered, for 20 minutes. Strain through fine strainer.

Chowder

3 cups fish stock
2 cups 2% milk
1 1/2 lb mussels (about 20)
1/2 cup white wine
salt
2 tbsp unsalted butter
2 tbsp extra-virgin olive oil
1 medium onion, diced
1 medium leek (white part only), diced
3 small carrots, diced
2 stalks celery, diced
6 new potatoes (golf ball size), cut in half
2 whole cloves garlic, smashed lightly with side of knife
1/2 tsp saffron
3 tbsp all-purpose flour
1 cup corn kernels (preferably sliced fresh from cob)
1/2 cup 35% cream
2 tbsp chopped fresh dill
1 tbsp minced garlic
salt and white pepper

In saucepan bring fish stock and milk to boil, stirring. Reduce heat and simmer, stirring, for 10 minutes; keep hot.

Meanwhile scrub mussels and remove beards. In heavy saucepan, combine mussels, wine and pinch salt; steam until mussels open. Strain, reserving liquor. Set mussels aside. (Discard any that have not opened.)

In large skillet, heat butter and oil over medium heat; sauté onion, leek, carrots, celery, new potatoes, whole garlic and saffron. Gradually stir in flour just until absorbed by butter and oil. Increase heat to high; add hot fish stock mixture, stirring constantly, until thickened.

Reduce heat and add corn, 35% cream, dill, minced garlic, and reserved liquor from mussels. Simmer just until vegetables are fork-tender. Add mussels and gently heat through. Taste and adjust seasoning with salt and white pepper if desired. Serves 6 as a first course.

Chef's wine suggestion — Dry Riesling, Cave Spring Cellars

Beaver Valley

ROASTED PEAR AND SWEET POTATO BISQUE WITH LOBSTER CAKES

Vineland Estates Winery Restaurant
Executive Chef: Mark Picone

In the early fall, when the harvest in the Niagara region is well underway, Chef Picone serves this hearty, thick, smooth-textured soup. He also suggests a variation substituting butternut squash, and salmon for the lobster. For simplicity, if you are not serving a fish cake, crème fraîche is wonderfully acidulous.

Bisque
1 tbsp olive oil
1 small sweet onion, chopped
2 stalks celery, chopped
1 carrot, chopped
3 cups chicken stock
1 bay leaf
1 tsp finely chopped fresh rosemary
salt and pepper
3 sweet potatoes (unpeeled)
3 Bosc pears
6 sprigs rosemary

In saucepan, heat oil over low heat; sauté onion, celery and carrot until soft. Add stock, bay leaf, rosemary and salt and pepper to taste; cook for 25 to 35 minutes. Remove bay leaf.

Place sweet potatoes and pears on baking tray and roast in 400°F oven for about 30 minutes or until soft. Let cool. Peel potatoes and pears. In food processor, purée potatoes, pears and stock mixture in batches. Return to saucepan over low heat and simmer until heated through. Season with salt and pepper to taste.

Lobster Cakes
2 lobsters
1 cup sugar snap peas, chopped
1 sweet red pepper, chopped
1 small red onion, chopped
1 egg, beaten
3 tbsp (approx) bread crumbs
1 tbsp sour cream
1 tsp Dijon mustard
salt and pepper
1 tbsp olive oil

Boil lobsters. Remove meat and chop.

In bowl, combine lobster meat, peas, red peppers, onions, egg, bread crumbs, sour cream, mustard and salt and pepper to taste. Form into 6 cakes and roll in more bread crumbs.

In nonstick skillet, heat oil over medium-high heat; sear patties, turning once, until brown.

Ladle bisque into shallow soup bowls; place lobster cake in centre of each bowl and garnish with rosemary sprig. Serves 6.

Chef's wine suggestion — Semi-Dry Riesling, 1995, Vineland Estates

Roasted Garlic and Potato Soup

ROASTED GARLIC AND POTATO SOUP

Rogues Restaurant
Executive Chef: Bevan Terry

This soup is a favourite of the patrons at Rogues, and you'll know why when you try it. The toppings can be varied. Chef Terry has also served it garnished with small poached shrimp and chopped chives. So be creative!

2 1/2 tsp olive oil
1 medium onion, finely chopped
1 small leek (white part only), finely chopped
8 cups chicken or vegetable stock
5 large potatoes, peeled and diced
1 bay leaf
12 cloves garlic
salt and pepper
plain yogurt
julienned cilantro

In large pot, heat 2 tsp of the oil over medium-low heat; sauté onion and leek until soft. Add chicken stock, potatoes and bay leaf; bring to boil. Simmer for 20 to 25 minutes.

Meanwhile, toss garlic cloves with remaining oil to coat; roast in 350°F oven for 20 to 25 minutes.

Add garlic to stock mixture. Remove bay leaf. Purée in 2 or 3 batches in food processor. Return to pot and gently heat through. Add salt and pepper to taste. Ladle into bowls. Garnish each with dollop of yogurt and cilantro. Serves 6 to 8 as a first course.

Chef's wine suggestion — Sauvignon Blanc, St. David Bench, 1995, Château des Charmes

Victoria Park, London

LEEK SOUP WITH BLUE CHEESE
Rinderlin's
Executive Chef: Jeff Pitchot

Chef Pitchot suggests serving this wonderful soup with croutons or baguette slices that have been topped with a Cheddar-mozzarella cheese blend and parsley, then toasted. For the daring, a dollop of whipped cream, sour cream or yogurt is nice as well.

1/2 cup julienned leek (light green to green part only)
2 tbsp butter, margarine or oil
2 cups coarsely chopped leeks (white and light green part only)
2 tbsp all-purpose flour
4 cups 10% cream or milk (or a combination of dairy and chicken stock)
salt and pepper
4 tsp shredded blue cheese

Blanch julienned leek in boiling water; set aside.

In saucepan, melt butter over medium heat; sauté chopped leeks until translucent. Blend in flour. Add cream. Bring to boil; simmer for about 15 minutes. Season with salt and pepper to taste.

Purée in food processor or blender, then strain into bowl.

To serve, place 1 tsp blue cheese in bottom of each of 4 soup bowls; ladle soup over top. Garnish with julienned leek. Serves 4 as a first course.

Chef's wine suggestion — Pinot Blanc, Kozelmann

CREAM OF SPINACH AND FETA SOUP
The Glenerin Inn
Executive Chef: John Harnett

Chef Harnett says that once you have made this basic cream soup, you can add any leaf vegetable and a variety of cheeses may be used, including white Cheddar, yellow Cheddar and Swiss.

2 bunches fresh spinach, stems removed
1 cup homemade or canned chicken stock
2 cups 2% milk
2 cups 10% cream
1/2 cup dry white wine
1 tbsp granulated sugar
2 tsp lemon rind
salt and pepper
3/4 cup crumbled feta cheese
6 sprigs watercress

Steam spinach just until wilted. In food processor or blender, combine spinach with chicken stock; purée until smooth. Pass mixture through sieve.

In saucepan over low heat, combine spinach purée, milk, cream, wine, sugar and lemon rind. Season with salt and pepper to taste. Simmer for 15 minutes or until flavours are well blended. Pass through sieve again. (Texture should be velvety.) Return to saucepan and heat to serve.

Ladle into 6 soup bowls and sprinkle with feta cheese. Garnish with watercress. Serves 6 as a first course.

Chef's wine suggestion — Dry Riesling, VQA, 1996, Cave Spring Cellars

Schoolhouse Restaurant

NIAGARA GAZPACHO
Wellington Court
Executive Chef: Erik Peacock

A summer delight! Cool, refreshing and full of fresh vegetables and flavour, this gazpacho can be made as mild or spicy as you wish.

4 1/2 cups tomato juice
1/4 cup finely diced sweet green pepper
1/4 cup finely diced yellow tomato
1/4 cup finely diced red onion
1/4 cup finely diced English cucumber
1/4 cup finely diced celery
juice of 1 lemon
large pinch salt
pinch white pepper
3 dashes Tabasco Sauce
2 dashes Worcestershire sauce

In bowl, combine tomato juice, green peppers, yellow tomatoes, onion, cucumber, celery, lemon juice, salt, white pepper, Tabasco Sauce and Worcestershire sauce. Refrigerate for at least 4 hours or overnight. Ladle into bowls. Serves 6.

Chef's wine suggestion — Carbernet Rose, Henry of Pelham

Niagara Gazpacho

Hearts of Romaine with Caramelized Onion Vinaigrette

SALADS

There was a time when salad meant iceberg lettuce or — if you were really a gourmet — romaine. But times have changed. Many of the recipes featured here use a combination of lettuces varying in taste and texture, and they are tossed in an array of flavour-packed dressings. Salads have the delightful diversity of either being served as a first course to a dinner party or served in a larger portion as a main course.

The trend toward warm salads can be seen in such recipes as Warm Goat Cheese Salad and Grilled Vegetables with Roasted Garlic Dressing from Janet Lynn's Bistro, or Warm Scallop and Portobello Salad from the Schoolhouse Country Inn Restaurant. I have included two Caesar Salad recipes: one is the tried-and-true classic Caesar Salad from Beild House Country Inn and the other is the deliciously unique Vodka Caesar Salad from the Prince of Wales Hotel.

Salads have come a long way since the days of iceberg lettuce, and the recipes included in this book show that progression.

Schoolhouse Restaurant, Belwood

WARM SCALLOP AND PORTOBELLO SALAD
The Schoolhouse Country Inn Restaurant
Owner/Chef: Peter Egger

I love delicious, easily prepared warm salads such as this one. Chef Egger suggests serving it for a light summer lunch or dinner main course. You can use shrimp instead of scallops or a combination of both.

1/4 cup olive oil
4 large portobello mushrooms, thinly sliced
1 clove garlic, minced
1 tbsp minced fresh gingerroot
1 shallot, minced
20 large sea scallops, halved
1/4 cup balsamic vinegar
mixed salad greens to serve 4
1 sprig fresh thyme
salt and pepper

In skillet, heat oil over medium-high heat; sauté mushrooms, garlic, ginger and shallots until tender. Add scallops and balsamic vinegar; cook just until scallops are firm and opaque.

Arrange greens in the centre of each of 4 plates. Using slotted spoon and reserving liquid in skillet, transfer scallops and mushrooms to top of greens. Stir thyme and salt and pepper to taste into skillet and bring to boil. Cook until reduced by one-quarter. Drizzle liquid over salad. Serves 4 as a first course.

Chef's wine suggestion — Riesling, Vineland Estates

Salad Deanna

The Glenerin Inn
Executive Chef: John Harnett

For a low-fat version, replace the mayonnaise and cream with low-fat plain yogurt and decrease the amount of lemon juice.

1 large head leaf lettuce
1 head radicchio
1/2 cup virgin olive oil
1/2 cup dry white wine
2 large cloves garlic, minced
1 1/2 lb medium shrimp, peeled and deveined
1 lb scallops
1 lb shark or other firm fish such as tuna or monkfish
5 kiwifruit, peeled and sliced
2 papayas, peeled and sliced
3 lemons, sliced
chopped fresh parsley
salt and pepper

Fish Mayonnaise

1 cup mayonnaise
1/3 cup 10% cream
3/4 cup lemon juice
2 tbsp grated onion
1/4 tsp Tabasco Sauce

Wash and dry leaf lettuce and radicchio; tear into pieces. Set aside in refrigerator.

In large skillet over medium-high heat, bring oil, wine and garlic to boil; simmer shrimp, scallops and fish for 3 to 4 minutes or until opaque. Drain seafood and keep warm in oven.

Fish Mayonnaise: In bowl, mix together mayonnaise, cream, lemon juice, onion and Tabasco Sauce.

Arrange bed of greens in centre of each of 6 dinner plates; top with shrimp, scallops and fish. Arrange sliced kiwi and papaya around edge. Garnish with lemon slices and parsley. Drizzle greens, shrimp, scallops and fish with fish mayonnaise. Serves 6 as a first course.

Chef's wine suggestion — Sauvignon Blanc, Château des Charmes

Niagara River, south of Niagara-on-the-Lake

1 cooked dungeness crab, 2 lb (to yield 8 to 10 oz crab meat)
4 ripe tomatoes, peeled, seeded and diced
10 basil leaves, coarsely shredded
2 cups baby salad greens
2 tbsp chopped fresh chives

Trim 6 of the artichokes, leaving some of the stalk intact. Pare down and remove choke from each artichoke. Place artichoke in water and rub with piece of lemon to expose flesh. Bring 4 cups salted water to boil; cook artichoke hearts until tender. Drain artichokes. Cut each artichoke into 6 pieces.

Toss with some of the vinaigrette.

Prepare remaining artichokes as above and let stand in water until ready to use. In deep saucepan, heat oil over medium-high heat to 325°F. Drain artichokes. Using mandoline or a sharp knife, thinly slice artichokes. Cook artichoke slices, a handful at a time, until crisp and few bubbles remain in oil. Drain well on paper towels. Season with salt and pepper to taste.

Orange Oil
1 cup orange juice
1 tbsp lemon juice
1/4 cup extra-virgin olive oil

In non-reactive saucepan over medium-high heat, stir together orange and lemon juices; reduce until almost syrupy (about 1/4 cup). Strain through fine strainer. Add oil and whisk lightly to combine.

To Assemble: In bowl, combine crab, boiled artichoke pieces, tomatoes and shredded basil. Season lightly with salt and pepper. Dress lightly with some of the vinaigrette.

Set aside 3 tbsp of the crab mixture; divide remaining crab mixture among each of 6 plates, placing in centre and spreading out slightly. Toss salad greens with remaining vinaigrette. Arrange on plates around crab mixture. Sprinkle reserved crab mixture over greens. Sprinkle artichoke chips around salad. Drizzle orange oil in border around greens. Sprinkle with chives. Serves 6.

Chef's wine suggestion — Riesling Dry, Cave Spring Cellars

Crab Salad with Artichokes

CRAB SALAD WITH ARTICHOKES
Rundles
Executive Chef: Neil Baxter

This is a very unique and superb-tasting salad. It features artichokes in two different ways — boiled and deep-fried into crispy chips.

Vinaigrette
1/2 cup light olive oil
3 tbsp lime juice
2 tbsp sherry vinegar
1 tbsp finely chopped shallots
1/2 tsp grated fresh gingerroot

Whisk together oil, lime juice, vinegar, shallots and ginger. Set aside.

9 artichokes
1 lemon, cut into quarters
4 cups corn oil
salt and pepper

HEARTS OF ROMAINE WITH CARAMELIZED ONION VINAIGRETTE
The Kiely Inn & Tapestries Restaurant
Executive Chef: Vincent Sica

This is a delicious salad and the presentation is lovely.

Onion Vinaigrette
1 cup olive oil + 1 tbsp
1 medium red onion, diced
4 shallots, diced
2 tbsp brown sugar
1/2 cup balsamic vinegar
salt and pepper

In nonstick skillet, heat 1 tbsp of the oil over medium-high heat; sauté onion and shallots until golden brown. Stir in sugar and remove from heat.

In slow stream, whisk remaining oil into balsamic vinegar. Add caramelized onions and salt and pepper to taste. Whisk again to blend thoroughly.

Salad
6 heads romaine lettuce (or, if available, hearts of romaine only)
12 slices pancetta
8 oz Parmigiano-Reggiano cheese, thinly shaved

Inglis Falls

Wash and thoroughly dry lettuce. Collect hearts of romaine, reserving green leaves for another use.

In skillet, fry pancetta until crisp. Set aside.

Arrange romaine attractively on 6 large plates. Pour vinaigrette over leaves. Top with 2 slices each pancetta; sprinkle with Parmesan cheese shavings. Serves 6 as a first course.

Chef's wine suggestion — Auxerrois, 1995, Inniskillin

CAESAR SALAD
Beild House Country Inn
Owner/Chef: Bill Barclay

Innkeepers Bill and Stephanie Barclay report that this classic Caesar salad remains a favourite. Serve with a barbecued steak and a full-bodied red wine.

1 1/2 heads romaine lettuce
1 large clove garlic, minced
1 tsp salt
1/3 cup olive oil
1 tbsp red wine vinegar
2 tsp dry mustard
2 tsp lemon juice
2 tsp anchovy paste or 1 anchovy fillet, finely chopped
1/4 tsp pepper
2 dashes Worcestershire sauce
1/4 cup freshly grated Parmesan cheese
1 egg

Wash and dry lettuce; tear into bite-size pieces.

Place garlic and salt in large wooden salad bowl; with fork, crush garlic into salt, working into bowl. Gradually add oil and work in with fork until combined. Gradually add vinegar, stirring until well blended. Add mustard, lemon juice, anchovy paste, pepper and Worcestershire sauce; mix well. Add Parmesan cheese and egg; mix thoroughly. Toss with lettuce. Serves 6.

Chef's tip: Garnish with garlic croutons.

Chef's wine suggestion — Trius Red, VQA, Hillebrand Estates

CANDY CANE BEET AND FETA CHEESE SALAD
The Wildwood Inn
Owner/Chef: Chris Woolf

Chef Woolf is fortunate to have a local organic farm supply him with vegetables throughout the year. If you cannot get candy cane or golden beets, red beets will do.

2 lb candy cane, golden or red beets
mixed salad greens to serve 6
2 tbsp extra-virgin olive oil
1 tbsp balsamic vinegar
salt and pepper
6 oz feta cheese
chopped fresh chives

Rinse beets but do not peel. In saucepan, cover beets with cold salted water and bring to boil; boil gently just until skins can be rubbed off easily. Let cool in water in saucepan. Remove skins, trim root ends and slice.

Toss greens with olive oil and arrange on each of 6 plates. Toss beet slices in balsamic vinegar; season with salt and pepper to taste. Arrange beets over greens and crumble feta cheese on top. Garnish with chopped chives. Serves 6.

Chef's wine suggestion — Rosé 1996, Cave Spring Cellars

ARUGULA SALAD WITH ROASTED PEARS AND DRIED CRANBERRIES
Anthony's
Owner/Chef: David Chapman

The nutty flavour of the arugula with the sautéed pears is a winning combination in this tasty salad.

2 ripe Bartlett pears
1 tbsp olive oil
2 large bunches arugula, washed and dried
1/2 cup dried cranberries

Peel and core pears; cut each into 12 wedges. In nonstick skillet, heat oil over high heat; sauté pears until light brown and crisp. Remove from pan and keep warm in oven.

Divide arugula among 6 salad plates. Arrange 4 pear wedges in fan shape at base of each plate. Sprinkle with dried cranberries. Drizzle with Anthony's vinaigrette. Serves 6.

Anthony's Vinaigrette
1 1/2 tbsp granulated sugar
1 tsp grainy mustard
1 tsp Dijon mustard
1/4 cup wine vinegar
3/4 cup olive or vegetable oil
salt and pepper

In large bowl, whisk together sugar, grainy mustard and Dijon mustard. Add half of the vinegar. Gradually whisk in oil until smooth. Add remaining vinegar and season with salt and pepper to taste.

Chef's tip: For best flavour, let vinaigrette stand in refrigerator overnight.

Chef's wine suggestion — Dry Riesling, Cave Spring Cellars

WARM GOAT CHEESE SALAD AND GRILLED VEGETABLES WITH ROASTED GARLIC DRESSING
Janet Lynn's Bistro
Owner/Chef: Janet Leslie

This fabulous salad is full of flavour. Serve for lunch with some crusty bread.

Roasted Garlic Dressing
3 egg yolks

2 tbsp Dijon mustard
2 tbsp roasted garlic (see tip below)
1 cup vegetable oil
1/4 cup lemon juice
dash Worcestershire sauce
dash Tabasco Sauce
salt and pepper

In food processor or blender, blend together briefly egg yolks, Dijon mustard and roasted garlic. While machine is running, gradually pour in oil. Blend in lemon juice, Worcestershire sauce, Tabasco Sauce and salt and pepper to taste. (If sauce is too thick, add a little hot water.)

Chef's tip: To roast garlic: cut bulb in half horizontally. Wrap in foil and bake in 400°F oven for 20 to 30 minutes or until very tender.

Warm Goat Cheese Salad and Grilled Vegetables
1 1/4 lb goat cheese (chèvre)
1 red onion, cut into 6 wedges
1 sweet red pepper, sliced lengthwise into 6 pieces
1 sweet yellow pepper, sliced lengthwise into 6 pieces
1 zucchini, cut into 1/2-inch-thick slices
1 eggplant, cut into 1/2-inch-thick slices
6 large mushrooms (preferably portobello), stems discarded

6 tbsp virgin olive oil
salt and pepper
1 tbsp chopped fresh thyme
torn mixed salad greens to serve 6
2 tbsp balsamic vinegar
1 tbsp chopped fresh parsley

Dipping thin knife in very hot water, cut goat cheese into 6 equal sections. Set aside.

Blanch onion wedges in boiling salted water for 2 minutes. Drain and refresh under cold water.

Arrange onions, red and yellow peppers, zucchini, eggplant and mushrooms on baking sheet; brush lightly with some of the olive oil. Season with salt and pepper to taste. Sprinkle with thyme. On grill over high heat, cook vegetables separately, about 2 minutes for peppers and about 4 minutes for the mushrooms, zucchini, eggplant and onion. While grilling, place grill tray of goat cheese on top rack of barbecue until warmed (not hot.)

Arrange bed of mixed greens in centre of each of 6 plates. Arrange grilled vegetables attractively around greens. Top greens with warm goat cheese. Drizzle greens and goat cheese with roasted garlic dressing. Whisk together remaining oil and balsamic vinegar; drizzle a little over grilled vegetables. Sprinkle with parsley and season with pepper to taste. Serves 6 as a first course.

Chef's wine suggestion — Gewürztraminer, Vineland Estates

Avon River, Stratford

INSALATA CAPRESE
da Caruso Ristorante
Owner/Chef: Diana Caruso

This deliciously simple summertime salad comes from the island of Capri.

6 medium vine-ripened tomatoes
4 large Fior di Latte cheeses or 18 bocconcini cheeses
romaine lettuce and radicchio to serve 6
1/2 cup extra-virgin olive oil
1/2 cup chopped fresh basil
salt and pepper

Slice tomatoes and cheese into 1/2-inch-thick slices. On large platter, arrange bed of romaine and radicchio. Alternate slices of tomatoes and cheese around platter. Drizzle olive oil over tomatoes and cheese. Sprinkle with basil and salt and pepper to taste. Serves 6.

Chef's wine suggestion — Chardonnay, VQA, VP Cellars

MIXED GREENS WITH POPPY SEED DRESSING
The Epicurean Fine Foods
Owner/Chef: Ruth Aspinall

Chef Aspinall is constantly asked for this recipe in her restaurant but has never revealed it until now. It's an amazingly versatile recipe. In berry season, she suggests adding some fresh raspberries or strawberries for great colour and taste. For another variation, decrease the vinegar to half, add 1/3 cup lime juice and a little more sugar and serve over fresh melon with a dollop of yogurt.

3/4 cup cider vinegar
1 1/2 tbsp granulated sugar
1 1/2 tbsp poppy seeds
1 1/2 tsp (heaping) dry mustard
1 1/2 tsp salt
1 1/2 tsp (heaping) onion powder
2 cups vegetable oil
torn mixed salad greens

In food processor or blender, combine vinegar, sugar, poppy seeds, mustard, salt and onion powder; pulse a few times to blend. With motor running, gradually pour in oil until well blended. Toss with greens. Makes about 2 cups.

Chef's wine suggestion — Cabernet Rose, VQA, 1996, Henry of Pelham

Countryside near Goderich

VODKA CAESAR SALAD
The Prince of Wales Hotel
Executive Chef: Ralf Bretzigheimer

I have included two Caesar salad recipes in this collection because they are so different. This colourful, tasty one puts a brand-new twist on the old classic.

Vinaigrette
1 cup Clamato juice
1/3 cup coarsely chopped red onions
2 1/2 tsp Worcestershire sauce
1 1/2 tsp Tabasco Sauce
1 1/2 tbsp vodka
1 tsp celery salt
3/4 tsp white pepper
1/2 tsp (approx) salt
1 1/2 cups olive oil
pepper

In blender or food processor, purée Clamato juice, onions, Worcestershire sauce, Tabasco Sauce, vodka, celery salt, white pepper and salt until fine. With motor running, gradually pour in oil and blend until emulsified. Let stand for 15 minutes to develop flavours. Add pepper to taste.

Salad
1/2 tomato baguette or regular baguette, sliced 1/4 inch thick
1/2 cup olive oil
1 1/2 heads romaine lettuce, torn into bite-sized pieces
2 tbsp finely diced tomato
2 tbsp finely diced celery
4 oz Parmesan cheese, thinly sliced
celery salt

Brush baguette slices with oil; place on a baking sheet. Bake in 300°F oven for 10 to 15 minutes or until bread is crisp.

In bowl, combine lettuce, tomatoes and celery; pour in vinaigrette and toss to coat. Arrange on plates or in shallow bowls and top with Parmesan cheese. Place toasted baguette slices alongside and sprinkle salad with little celery salt. Serves 6.

Chef's wine suggestion — Chardonnay, Cave Spring Cellars

Vodka Caesar Salad

Grilled Venison Chop

ENTRÉES

Choosing the recipes for this book was truly an enjoyable experience. Each of the chefs I worked with had his or her own unique style which is reflected in the wide range of creative dishes.

Because southwestern Ontario is so bountiful, all the chefs work with their local regional producers and use only the freshest ingredients. This section includes entrées for both family meals and special-occasion entertaining. A broad range of selections is offered, including poultry, lamb, beef, pork, game, seafood, pasta, and vegetarian dishes.

The Penne Calabrese or Osso Bucco from Trattoria Il Timone can make a hearty family dinner or be served at a casual gathering of friends. Spoil your guests with a sensational seafood dish such as Linguine Mare from da Caruso Ristorante or Grilled Tuna with Chilled Olive Salad from Benmiller Inn. On the light vegetarian side, the Cheese Soufflé from Enver's or the Grilled Vegetable and Tofu Tortes or Lentil and Vegetable Tortes from the Wildflower Restaurant make tasty, healthy meals. Enjoy!

GRILLED TUNA WITH CHILLED OLIVE SALAD
Benmiller Inn
Executive Chef: Derek Griffiths

Chef Griffiths suggests grilling asparagus spears at the same time as grilling the tuna steak for a perfect accompaniment to this entrée.

Chilled Olive Salad
1 cup green olives, pitted and diced
1 cup black olives, pitted and diced
1 small sweet red pepper, seeded and diced
2 garlic cloves, minced
rind (thinly julienned) and juice of 1 lemon
1 tsp dried oregano
1/2 red onion, diced

In large bowl, combine green and black olives, red pepper, garlic, lemon rind and juice, oregano and onion; mix well. Cover and refrigerate to chill well before serving. Serves 6.

Grilled Tuna
6 tuna steaks, each 5 oz

Marinade
1 cup extra-virgin olive oil
1/4 cup lemon juice
1 tbsp crushed black peppercorns
1/2 tsp garlic powder or 1 tsp chopped garlic
1/2 large red onion, diced

Marinade: Combine oil, lemon juice, peppercorns, garlic powder and onion. Place tuna steaks in glass baking dish; pour marinade over top. Cover and marinate in the refrigerator for at least 1/2 hour or for up to 2 hours.

Place tuna steaks on barbecue grill over high heat; cook for 2 to 3 minutes; turn and grill for another 2 to 3 minutes or until medium-rare.
Place steaks on individual serving plates; top each with generous amount of chilled olive salad.

Chef's wine suggestion — Cabernet Merlot, Stoney Ridge

ROASTED SEA BASS WITH BALSAMIC BEURRE-BLANC SAUCE
Enver's
Owner/Chef: Enver Bismallah

This sea bass is easy to prepare yet it's elegant enough to serve for a dinner party.

6 sea bass fillets, each 6 to 8 oz
drizzle olive oil
1/4 lb unsalted butter
1/2 cup white wine
1/2 cup 35% cream
1/4 cup balsamic vinegar
juice of 1 lemon

Place sea bass in roasting pan and drizzle with oil. Roast in 400°F oven for 15 minutes.
In saucepan over medium heat, melt butter; stir in wine, cream, balsamic vinegar and lemon juice. Bring to boil and reduce by half, stirring often. Spoon sauce over fish to serve. Serves 6.

Chef's wine suggestion — Proprietors' Reserve, Henry of Pelham

STRIPED SEA BASS WITH LEMON PEPPER BUTTER SAUCE AND CORN AND POTATO RISOTTO
The Kiely Inn & Tapestries Restaurant
Executive Chef: Vincent Sica

The lemon pepper butter sauce is lovely with this delicate sea bass entrée. Instead of using frozen corn and searing in a hot pan, you can barbecue fresh corn on the cob on the grill and slice it from the cob when cooled.

6 striped sea bass fillets, each 6 to 8 oz
salt and pepper
1 cup all-purpose flour
1/4 cup vegetable oil

Lemon Pepper Butter
1/4 cup white wine
1 tsp lemon juice
1/2 lb unsalted butter, cubed
pepper

Striped Sea Bass

Lemon Pepper Butter: In heavy saucepan heat wine and lemon juice over medium-high heat; reduce to about 2 tbsp. Let cool slightly.

Reduce heat to very low and whisk in butter 1 cube at a time, whisking each until well blended. Continue until all butter is blended and mixture is velvety. Pour sauce into bowl and add pepper to taste. Set aside.

Sprinkle fish with salt and pepper to taste, then dredge in flour.

In ovenproof skillet, heat oil over medium-high heat; fry fish, turning once, for 2 to 3 minutes or until golden yellow.

Transfer to 450°F oven and continue cooking for 8 to 10 minutes or until opaque and flakes easily when tested with fork.

Risotto

8 to 10 medium Yukon Gold potatoes, peeled and diced
1 cup cooked arborio rice
2 tsp vegetable oil
1 cup frozen corn
1 cup homemade fish stock or fish bouillon
saffron (a few strands)
1 package fresh spinach (10 oz), chopped
salt and pepper

Meanwhile, in pot of boiling water, cook potatoes until tender. Drain and set aside. Cook rice according to package directions.

In very hot skillet, heat 1 tsp oil; cook corn until appears grilled.

Meanwhile, in separate skillet heat remaining oil over medium-high heat, fry diced potatoes and rice for 2 to 3 minutes or until heated through. Add corn, fish stock, saffron, spinach and salt and pepper to taste; cook for 2 to 3 minutes.

Place 1 fillet on each plate; spoon lemon pepper butter over top. Serve with potato risotto. Serves 6.

Chef's tip: For a richer taste, add butter and Parmesan cheese to risotto.

Chef's wine suggestion — Pinot Blanc, Konzelmann

TROUT BAKED IN APPLE CIDER
Langdon Hall
Executive Chef: Louise Duhamel

Chef Duhamel comments that using apple cider instead of traditional wine provides a pleasant fruity flavour with a note of acidity.

2 tbsp vegetable oil
1 medium onion, cut into 1/8-inch-thick slices
1 carrot, cut into 1/8-inch-thick slices
4 trout fillets, each 6 oz
1 cup apple cider
salt and pepper
1/4 cup apple cider vinegar
2 tbsp liquid honey
2 tbsp 35% cream
1/4 cup unsalted butter

In saucepan, heat oil over medium-low heat; sauté onions until soft. Let cool. Blanch carrots in boiling water; let cool.

Place fish on greased baking pan. Top with carrots, onions, apple cider and salt and pepper to taste; cover with foil. Bake in 400°F oven for 8 to 10 minutes or until fish is opaque and flakes easily when tested with fork.

Pour juices from fish into small saucepan over high heat; cook until reduced to 1/2 cup. Add cider vinegar. Cook until reduced to 1/2 cup. Add honey and cream. Reduce again to 1/2 cup. Whisk in butter and adjust seasoning to taste.

Spoon sauce over trout to serve. Serves 4.

Chef's wine suggestion — Gewürztraminer, Henry of Pelham or Chardonnay Reserve, Paul Bosc, Château des Charmes

FILLET OF LAKE TROUT WITH MORELS AND FIDDLEHEADS ON LINGUINE
The Little Inn of Bayfield
Executive Chef: Jamie Stearns

This superb entrée is a grand way to enjoy fresh lake trout and fiddleheads when they're in season.

6 lake trout fillets, (small bones removed as much as possible), each 6 oz
salt and pepper
1 tbsp butter
1 tbsp olive oil
2 shallots, finely diced
18 large morels or portobello mushrooms, cut into bite-sized pieces

Bayfield

1 cup Chardonnay
1 cup 35% cream
1 tbsp Cognac
2 sprigs thyme
1 sprig rosemary
salt and white pepper

Pasta
1 1/2 lb (750 g) linguine
1 tbsp butter
1 tbsp olive oil
1 shallot, finely chopped
1 cup chicken stock
1/2 cup 35% cream

Vegetables
60 fiddleheads
2 tbsp butter
1 shallot, finely chopped
1 clove garlic, minced
salt and pepper

Season fish fillets on both sides with salt and pepper. In ovenproof skillet, heat butter and oil over medium-high heat; sear fish on both sides. Transfer to 350°F oven and bake for 15 minutes.

Add shallots to pan; cook until translucent. Add mushrooms; sauté until tender. Remove from pan.

Deglaze pan with Chardonnay. Add cream and Cognac and reduce until slightly thickened. Add mushroom mixture, thyme, rosemary and salt and white pepper to taste. Keep warm. (Remove thyme and rosemary before serving.)

Pasta: Cook pasta in boiling salted water until al dente. Drain and return to pot. In skillet, heat butter and oil; sauté shallots briefly. Add chicken stock and cream and cook until slightly thickened. Toss with pasta.

Vegetables: Blanch fiddleheads in boiling water for 3 minutes. In clean skillet, heat butter over medium heat; sauté fiddleheads, shallots and garlic until warmed through. Season with salt and pepper to taste.

To serve, make pasta nest in centre of each of 6 plates. Place trout on top. Spoon sauce over fish, dividing mushrooms equally. Place fiddlehead mixture attractively around perimeter of plate. Serves 6.

Chef's wine suggestion — Chardonnay, VQA, 1995, Saint David's Bench, Château des Charmes

Fillet of Lake Trout

Forks of the Credit River

SESAME-CRUSTED SEARED SALMON WITH CITRUS BUTTER
La Cachette
Owner/Chef: Alain Levesque

This delicious salmon dish has a crispy coating with a delicate combination of flavours.

6 salmon fillets, each 6 oz
1 cup milk

Stratford Provincial County Courthouse

1/4 cup sesame seeds
1/4 cup olive oil
1 cup dry white wine
1 tbsp finely chopped shallots
1 tbsp lime juice
1/2 cup 35% cream
3 tbsp butter
salt and pepper

Soak salmon in milk for five minutes. Spread sesame seeds in shallow dish or bowl; roll salmon in sesame seeds until coated well.

In large skillet, heat oil over high heat; cook salmon on both sides until light brown on outside and opaque throughout. Transfer to ovenproof platter and keep warm in oven.

In saucepan over medium heat, combine wine, shallots and lime juice; cook, stirring often, for 5 minutes. Add cream and cook until sauce begins to thicken. Whisk in butter, 1 tbsp at a time. Season with salt and pepper to taste. Spoon citrus butter over salmon to serve. Serves 6.

Chef's wine suggestion — Riesling, Lakeview Estates

BAKED ATLANTIC SALMON WITH LEMON CREAM SAUCE AND CREAMY RISOTTO

The Wildflower Restaurant
Owner/Chef: Wolfgang Sterr

Chef Sterr recommends serving this salmon and risotto dish with a mixture of colourful vegetables, such as carrots, green beans, and sweet red and green peppers. For more taste, blanch vegetables, then sauté in butter and chopped fresh herbs.

6 Atlantic salmon fillets, each 6 oz

Garlic and Herb Crust

5 slices white bread
3/4 cup butter
3 tsp chopped fresh herbs (cilantro, dill, basil)
1 tsp minced garlic
1 tsp minced shallots
salt and pepper

In food processor, pulse bread until fine.

In bowl, whip butter until soft. Add herbs, garlic and shallots; mix thoroughly. Blend in bread and salt and pepper to taste.

Spread mixture about 1/2 inch thick over each salmon fillet. Bake in 450°F oven for 10 to 12 minutes or until golden brown.

Lemon Cream Sauce

1 tsp olive oil
1/2 tsp minced shallot
2/3 cup dry white wine
juice of 1 lemon
1 1/2 cups 35% cream
1/2 tsp chopped dill
salt and pepper

In nonstick skillet, heat oil over medium-high heat; sauté shallots for 1 minute. Add wine and lemon juice and reduce by half. Add cream, dill and salt and pepper to taste; bring to boil. Remove from heat until serving; warm gently.

Creamy Risotto

2 1/2 to 3 1/2 cups vegetable stock
2/3 cup dry white wine
1 tsp olive oil
1 tsp minced garlic
1 tsp minced shallot
1 cup arborio rice
1 tbsp butter or margarine
1 tsp freshly grated Parmesan cheese
salt and pepper

In saucepan, stir stock with wine. Bring to boil; reduce heat to low and keep warm.

In large nonstick skillet, heat olive oil over medium-high heat; sauté garlic and shallots for 1 minute. Add rice and sauté for 1 minute. Add warm stock mixture 1/2 cup at a time, stirring until each addition is absorbed. Cook for 15 to 20 minutes. Rice should be creamy and firm, not runny.

Just before serving, stir in butter, Parmesan cheese and salt and pepper to taste. Ladle lemon cream sauce on each of 6 plates; place piece of salmon on top. Spoon risotto onto each plate. Serves 6.

Chef's wine suggestion — Chardonnay Reserve, 1995, Strewn

Salmon Monette

SALMON MONETTE
The Church Restaurant
Owner/Chef: Sheldon Russell

Salmon Monette is fresh Atlantic salmon with lemon, ginger, jasmine rice and toasted sesame wrapped in nori and steamed. It is served with pickled ginger and Japanese dipping sauce. This unique dish is Chef Russell's version of cooked sushi for the Western world. He presented it to Richard Monette, artistic director of the Stratford Festival, for his 50th birthday celebration.

Sushi
5 tbsp granulated sugar
5 tbsp rice vinegar
2 tsp salt
1 cup jasmine rice, washed
1 1/4 cups cold water
1 1/2 tbsp sesame oil
1 tbsp toasted sesame seeds
1/2 tbsp lemon rind, blanched and chopped
6 sheets nori (dried seaweed)
soy sauce
wasabi (Japanese horseradish), optional
6 skinless Atlantic salmon fillets (centre section only), each 5 oz

In saucepan over low heat, combine sugar, rice vinegar and salt; cook until sugar and salt are dissolved. Cool quickly by setting pan in cold water.

Combine rice and water in metal or glass bowl small enough to fit in large saucepan with lid. Pour in enough water to come halfway up side of bowl; bring to boil over high heat. Reduce heat to medium-low and cover. Simmer until water is absorbed and rice is cooked but still chewy and sticky. Let cool for 15 minutes. Transfer rice to large bowl. Gently stir in just enough of the sugar mixture to make rice stick together. Stir in the sesame oil, sesame seeds and lemon rind.

Brush one sheet of nori lightly with soy sauce. Smear small amount of wasabi (if using) in centre. Turn nori so that 1 corner is facing you. Spoon some of the rice horizontally across centre, leaving 1 1/2-to 2-inch border at each end. (Rice should be about 1/2 inch deep.) Place salmon fillet on top of rice. Tuck rice under

salmon to make sausage shape. Fold in side corners of nori. (You will be folding over the ends of the salmon fillet.) Fold corner closest to you over salmon towards top corner. Roll up firmly. Wrap in plastic wrap.

Place salmon rolls in plastic wrap on Chinese or conventional steamer; steam gently for 15 to 20 minutes or until salmon feels firm but is still a little rare. Remove rolls and unwrap. Slicing on bias, trim into 3 pieces.

Dipping Sauce
2 tbsp granulated sugar
2 tbsp sherry
2 tbsp soy sauce
2 tbsp chicken stock
2 tsp rice vinegar
1 tsp sesame oil
1 tbsp cornstarch

In saucepan, combine sugar, sherry, soy sauce, stock, vinegar and oil; bring to boil. Dissolve cornstarch in 2 tsp water and stir into pan. Reduce heat to low and simmer for 2 to 3 minutes. Serves 6.

Chef's tip: Chef Russell serves this with stir-fried vegetables in the centre, with the salmon arranged around the vegetables like the spokes of a wheel, sautéed shiitake mushrooms in between and the dipping sauce ladled over the mushrooms.

Chef's wine suggestion — Riesling, Johannesburg, VQA, Konzelmann

Stratford

PAELLA VALENCIA
Anthony's
Owner/Chef: David Chapman

You can vary the seafood in this wonderful classic dish. Chef Chapman serves the paella right out of the paella pan at the table and recommends you do the same at home for maximum presentation effect.

3 slices bacon, diced
1 sweet red pepper, coarsely diced
1 sweet green pepper, coarsely diced
1/2 red onion, coarsely diced
8 cups chicken stock
2 tbsp tomato paste
1 tbsp minced garlic
1/2 tbsp dried oregano
large pinch saffron
1 cup long-grain rice
2 boneless skinless chicken breasts, cut in pieces
1 spicy cooked smoked sausage, sliced
8 mussels
4 cherrystone or littleneck clams
8 scallops
8 large shrimp, peeled and deveined
2 squid, cut in rings
2 tbsp frozen green peas (thawed)
1 small jar (2 oz) pimientos, drained and thickly sliced

In large saucepan, fry bacon until just cooked (not crisp). Add red and green peppers and onion; sauté briefly until fragrant. Set aside 1 cup of the chicken stock. Add remaining stock to pan, along with tomato paste, garlic, oregano and saffron; bring to boil. Reduce heat and simmer for about 10 minutes. (Can be prepared to this point and refrigerated, covered, for up to 2 days.)

Transfer stock mixture to paella pan or wok or large skillet (sides at least 2 inches high); bring stock to boil. Stir in rice; reduce heat and simmer, stirring, for about 5 minutes.

Stir in chicken and sausage; cover and simmer for about 5 minutes, stirring occasionally. Meanwhile, scrub mussels and remove beards. Discard any mussels or clams that do not close when tapped. Place mussels, clams, scallops, shrimp and squid on top of rice mixture; cover and steam, turning seafood halfway through cooking, for about 5 minutes or until clams and mussels have opened and shrimps and scallops are opaque. Discard any clams and mussels that have not opened.

To serve, sprinkle paella with peas and place sliced pimientos on top. Heat remaining stock and pour over top to moisten (rice will absorb the liquid). Spoon onto individual plates. Serves 6.

Chef's wine suggestion — Cabernet Franc, Harrow Winery

Caledon countryside

LINGUINE MARE
da Caruso Ristorante
Owner/Chef: Diana Caruso

Chef Caruso says that variations of this dish are found throughout Italy. You can create your own by substituting different shellfish, such as manila clams or lobster.

1/2 lb each mussels, clams, scallops, shrimp and squid
1 cup olive oil
12 cloves garlic, minced
1 small onion, minced
1 cup white wine
2 cans (each 19 oz) Italian tomatoes
1 1/2 lb (750 g) linguine pasta
1/4 cup unsalted butter (optional)
1 tsp crushed chili pepper (optional)
salt and pepper
1/2 cup chopped fresh parsley

Scrub mussels and remove beards. Clean clams and scallops. Peel and devein shrimp. Cut squid into rings.

In large skillet or saucepan, heat oil over medium heat; sauté garlic and onion until translucent. Add mussels, clams and wine; cook, covered, over high heat until they open. (Discard any that do not open.) Add remaining seafood and tomatoes; bring to boil. Cook over medium-high heat for about 5 minutes or until sauce is thickened slightly.

Meanwhile, cook linguine in pot of boiling salted water until al dente. Drain and add to sauce; mix well. Stir in butter (if using), chili pepper (if using) and salt and pepper to taste. Garnish with parsley. Serves 6.

Chef's wine suggestion — Baco Noir, VQA, Henry of Pelham

LINGUINE WITH SHRIMPS AND SCALLOPS
The Elm Hurst Inn
Executive Chef: Darrell Stewart

This colourful pasta dish is light and fresh-tasting.

1 large bunch asparagus
1 1/2 lb (750 g) linguine pasta
3/4 cup olive oil
1 lb shrimp, peeled and deveined (tail intact)
1 lb scallops
1 1/2 cups sliced wild mushrooms (shiitake, portobello or oyster)
3 small cloves garlic, minced
1/3 cup white wine
1/4 cup sliced scallions
2 tbsp chopped mixed fresh herbs (parsley, basil, thyme)
3/4 cup chopped seeded tomatoes
3/4 cup freshly grated Parmesan cheese
salt and pepper

Cut asparagus into 2-inch pieces and blanch in boiling water; set aside. In large pot of boiling salted water, cook linguine until al dente; drain and return to pot.

In skillet, heat oil over medium heat; sauté shrimp just until opaque. Remove with slotted spoon and place on warmed plate; cover with foil and set aside. Cook scallops in same manner and set aside on the same plate.

To liquid in skillet, add mushrooms, asparagus and garlic; sauté over medium heat for 1 minute. Add wine, scallions and herbs; heat through. Pour sauce over linguine; add tomatoes, Parmesan cheese and salt and pepper to taste. Toss well. Divide among pasta bowls or plates and place shrimps and scallops attractively on top. Serve with extra Parmesan cheese on the side. Serves 6.

Chef's wine suggestion — Chardonnay, 1996, Cave Spring Cellars

PENNE CALABRESE

Trattoria Il Timone
Executive Chef: Michel Fronteddu

This sauce is easily prepared and tastes fantastic. The long, slow cooking makes the sausage very tender.

2 lb sweet Italian sausage, cut into 1/2-inch pieces
4 cups crushed plum tomatoes
1 sweet red pepper, diced
1 sweet yellow pepper, diced
1 jalapeño pepper, thinly sliced
1 1/2 lb (750 g) penne
olive oil

In saucepan over low heat, combine sausage, tomatoes, red and yellow peppers and jalapeño pepper; cook, covered, for 2 to 3 hours.

In separate saucepan, cook penne until al dente. Drain. Toss with a little olive oil. Divide penne among 6 warmed plates and spoon sauce over top. Serves 6.

Chef's wine suggestion — Cabernet Sauvignon, Château des Charmes

SWEET POTATO GNOCCHI WITH GRILLED VEGETABLES AND GOAT CHEESE

Rogues Restaurant
Executive Chef: Bevan Terry

These sweet potato gnocchi are outstanding with the grilled vegetables and goat cheese. The vegetables can be varied; use any seasonal fare that grills well. Note that it is important to mix the pasta ingredients with your hands.

Pasta

3 medium sweet potatoes (unpeeled)
3 egg yolks
1 cup all-purpose flour
salt and pepper
3/4 cup goat cheese (chèvre), crumbled
2 tsp chopped fresh basil
1 tsp chopped fresh sage
salt and pepper

Roast sweet potatoes in 350°F oven for about 45 minutes or until very tender. Remove skins and let cool. Using hands, combine potatoes, egg yolks, flour and salt and pepper to taste just until mixed. Cover and refrigerate for 1 hour.

Sweet Potato Gnocchi

On lightly floured surface, divide dough into 8 pieces. Using hand, roll 1 piece into long 1/2-inch-thick cylinder. Cut into 1/2-inch-long pieces. Repeat with remaining dough pieces. Dust with flour; cover and refrigerate until ready to use.

Grilled Vegetables
1 large eggplant
1 Bermuda onion
1 carrot
1 sweet red pepper
2 stalks celery
12 portobellini mushrooms
3 tsp olive oil
1 tsp balsamic vinegar

Cut eggplant, onion, carrot, red pepper, celery and mushrooms into bite-size pieces. Toss with oil and balsamic vinegar; transfer to grill basket and place on barbecue over high heat; cook until tender. Cover and keep warm. Turn basket over occasionally.

Meanwhile, in large pot of heavily salted boiling water, cook gnocchi until they float to the surface, and continue to cook for 30 seconds. Drain well. Return gnocchi to pot and mix with grilled vegetables. Toss with goat cheese, basil and sage. Season with salt and pepper to taste. Serves 6.

Chef's wine suggestion — Riesling Reserve, 1995, Strewn Vineyards

BAKERS' CHICKEN VERMICELLI
Blackshop Restaurant & Lounge
Executive Chefs: Alex Vetrovsky and Ladislav Kilian

This entrée is easily prepared and tastes superb.

1/3 cup fresh bread crumbs
1 lb (500 g) vermicelli pasta, spaghettini or other pasta
1/3 cup extra-virgin olive oil
3 medium boneless skinless chicken breasts cut into 1/2 inch cubes
6 slices pancetta or bacon, sliced into 1/2 inch strips
7 cloves garlic, crushed
pinch pepper

Caledon

6 medium portobello mushrooms, sliced 1/2 inch thick
2 cups chicken stock
chopped fresh herbs

Toast bread crumbs under broiler until golden. Set aside.

In pot of boiling water, cook vermicelli until al dente. Set aside.

Meanwhile, in large skillet over high heat, heat oil; cook chicken and pancetta until chicken is golden brown. Add garlic and pepper; sauté until garlic is golden brown and chicken is no longer pink inside. Add mushrooms and stock; cook over high heat for 1 minute to reduce stock. Add pasta and toss. Serve on warmed plates. Garnish with toasted bread crumbs and herbs. Serves 4 to 6.

Chef's wine suggestion — Pinot Noir, Inniskillin

Harbour, Port Stanley

PAN-SEARED BREAST OF CHICKEN WITH BRAISED RUBY CHARD AND RHUBARB WINE

Kettle Creek Inn
Executive Chef: Frank Hubert

The chicken set on top of the ruby chard is a lovely combination. The sauce is deliciously subtle. Serve with your favourite vegetable and potato.

1/4 cup extra-virgin olive oil
6 boneless skinless chicken breasts, each 6 oz
1 large bunch ruby chard or Swiss chard
1 1/8 cups rhubarb wine* or dry pink Zinfandel
1/2 cup unsalted butter
1 tbsp crushed black peppercorns
2 tbsp chopped shallots

In large nonstick skillet, heat oil over medium-high heat; sear chicken until golden brown.

Wash, dry and shred chard. Place in small roasting pan along with chicken and half of the wine. Roast, covered, in 400°F oven for about 10 minutes or until chicken is no longer pink inside. Transfer chicken and chard to plate and keep warm. Place pan over medium-high heat; pour in remaining wine and cook until reduced by half. Whisk in butter, peppercorns and shallots. Remove from heat.

Divide chard among 6 plates; place chicken breasts on top and pour sauce over top. Serves 6.

* Rhubarb wine is produced by Quai du Vin Winery, a local winery

Chef's wine suggestion — Baco Noir, VQA, Pelee Island Winery

GRAIN-FED CHICKEN WITH HERBED CREAM CHEESE AND FRESH TOMATO SAUCE
Keystone Alley Café
Owner/Chef: Sheldon Russell

Chef Russell serves this delicious chicken with porcini mushroom risotto and grilled mixed vegetables.

6 grain-fed boneless chicken breasts (skin on), each 7 oz
9 oz cream cheese
1/2 cup chopped mixed fresh herbs (tarragon, thyme, parsley, oregano, chives and chervil)
2 tbsp olive oil
salt and pepper

Fresh Tomato Sauce
1 tbsp olive oil
4 shallots, chopped
2 cloves garlic, crushed
7 fresh ripe tomatoes, seeded and chopped
1/2 cup dry white wine
1/4 cup chicken stock
6 oregano leaves, chopped
1 sprig each thyme and tarragon
1/2 bay leaf
salt and pepper

Place 1 chicken breast skin side down on work surface. Using sharp knife, remove fillet. Make shallow incision lengthwise along breast. Carefully work knife toward sides of breasts without cutting completely. Make horizontal incisions along top and bottom of lengthwise incision, creating flaps. Open up flaps. Gently flatten chicken between 2 pieces of plastic wrap, being careful not to separate. In same manner, flatten fillet. Repeat with remaining chicken breasts.

In food processor, blend cream cheese with herbs until smooth.

Spoon equal amounts of cream cheese mixture along centre of each breast, shaping lengthwise. Place slightly flattened fillet on top. To close, pull flaps over fillet.

In large nonstick skillet, heat oil over medium-high heat; place chicken in skillet skin side down and brown on 1 side only. Transfer, skin side up, to ovenproof platter or baking sheet; roast in 375°F oven for 20 to 25 minutes or until no longer pink inside. Let stand for 10 minutes.

Fresh tomato sauce: Meanwhile, in skillet, heat oil over medium heat; sauté shallots until soft. Add garlic and cook for 1 minute. Add tomatoes, wine, stock, oregano, thyme, tarragon, bay leaf and salt and pepper to taste; cook for 15 to 20 minutes. Discard sprigs of thyme and tarragon and bay leaf. Spoon over chicken to serve. Serves 6.

Chef's wine suggestion — Aligote, VQA, Château des Charmes

CHICKEN WITH HONEY AND POMMERY MUSTARD GLAZE
La Cachette
Owner/Chef: Alain Levesque

This "comfort food" chicken recipe is ideally accompanied by mashed potatoes and your favourite vegetable.

6 boneless skinless chicken breasts
salt and pepper
1/4 cup olive oil
1 tbsp unsalted butter
1 tbsp finely chopped shallots
3 tbsp liquid honey
1 cup demi-glaze
3 tbsp Pommery mustard (or grainy old-fashioned mustard)

Season chicken with salt and pepper to taste. In large skillet, heat oil over medium heat; cook chicken breasts until light brown on outside. Place on ovenproof plate and roast in 350°F oven for about 10 minutes or until no longer pink inside.

Add butter and shallots to skillet; sauté over low heat for 2 minutes, stirring to scrape up any brown bits from bottom of skillet. Add honey; cook until slightly caramelized (light brown). Increase heat to medium and add demi-glaze; cook, stirring often, for 5 minutes. Blend in mustard and salt and pepper to taste. To serve, spoon honey mustard glaze over chicken. Serves 6.

Chef's wine suggestion — Baco Noir, Henry of Pelham

Stratford Provincial County Courthouse

BREAST OF CHICKEN WITH GOAT CHEESE AND SUN-DRIED TOMATO JUS
The Wildwood Inn
Owner/Chef: Chris Woolf

Chef Woolf suggests serving potatoes and sautéed spinach with this scrumptious chicken entrée.

6 boneless chicken breasts (skin on), each 6 oz
1 tbsp basil pesto (homemade or purchased)
6 oz goat cheese
3 tbsp olive oil
1/2 cup dry white wine
1 cup strong chicken stock
4 tbsp cold unsalted butter
2 tbsp chopped oil-packed sun-dried tomatoes

Place 1 chicken breast skin side down on work surface. Using sharp knife, remove fillet. Make shallow incision lengthwise along breast. Carefully work knife toward sides of breast without cutting completely. Make horizontal incisions along top and bottom of lengthwise incision, creating flaps. Open up flaps. Gently flatten fillet between 2 pieces of plastic wrap. Repeat with remaining chicken breasts.

Spread pesto on inside of chicken breasts. Place 1 oz of goat cheese in centre of each breast, shaping lengthwise. Place slightly flattened fillet on top. To close, pull flaps over fillet.

In large ovenproof skillet, heat 2 tbsp of the oil over high heat. Brush skinless side of breasts with remaining oil. Place breasts in skillet, skin side down, and brown lightly on 1 side only. Transfer to top rack of 375°F oven and cook for about 15 minutes or until no longer pink inside. Remove from skillet and keep warm.

Meanwhile, drain fat from skillet. Deglaze skillet with wine; cook until reduced by one-quarter. Add stock and reduce by another one-quarter. While still boiling, whisk in butter, then remove from heat. Pass through strainer into bowl. Toss in sun-dried tomatoes. To serve, spoon sauce over chicken breasts. Serves 6.

Chef's wine suggestion — Chardonnay Reserve, 1996, Inniskillin

BEBEK BETUTU (ROAST DUCK)
Bhima's Warung International
Owner/Chef: Paul Boehmer

On the island of Bali, Indonesia, this dish is reserved for special occasions and cooked slowly all day by burying the packaged bird in the sand and building a fire out of coconut husks on top of it. The fresh spices and banana leaves are available in southeast Asian grocery stores. Chef Boehmer suggests accompanying this full-flavoured duck with a sweet and sour fruit sauce. Tamarind peach works well with the richness of the dish. He also recommends serving it with simple steamed Thai rice and a green vegetable such as spinach.

1 cup ground candlenuts or almonds
1 tbsp fresh turmeric
1 tbsp finely grated fresh galangal
1 tbsp finely grated fresh lemongrass
1 tbsp minced garlic
1 tbsp chopped shallots
1 tsp chopped Thai (bird) chilies
1 tsp ground coriander seeds
1 tsp nutmeg
1 tsp cinnamon
1/2 tsp ground cloves
1/2 tsp ground cardamom
1/2 tsp salt
1 tbsp vegetable oil
1 Chinese duck
banana leaves (enough to wrap duck, about 2 feet)

In food processor, chop nuts, turmeric, galangal, lemongrass, garlic, shallots and chilies until very fine. Add coriander seeds, nutmeg, cinnamon, cloves, cardamom and salt; process until combined. In a nonstick skillet, heat oil over low heat; cook spice mixture until fragrant, 4 to 5 minutes. Let cool.

Wash duck under cold running water. Remove neck and giblets and pat dry inside and out. Using hands and small sharp knife, loosen skin all the way around duck, being careful not to tear it. Spread spice mixture under skin, on top of skin and in cavity of duck.

Wrap duck in banana leaves, then in foil. Bake in 350°F oven for 3 1/2 hours. Carefully remove foil and banana leaves, saving leaves for presentation. Increase temperature to 475°F; cook duck 10 to 12 minutes longer or until skin is brown and crisp. Line serving platter with reserved banana leaves; place duck on top. Serves 2.

Chef's wine suggestion — Gewürztraminer, Stoney Ridge

Countryside near Goderich

BARBECUED BREAST OF DUCK ACCENTED WITH COCONUT & ACCOMPANIED WITH GRILLED VEGETABLES
Benmiller Inn
Executive Chef: Derek Griffiths

Chef Griffiths recommends serving this duck dish with his fabulous barbecue sauce and grilled vegetables. The barbecue sauce also goes well with salmon or any kind of meat or poultry. The recipe makes about 4 cups of sauce, which can be refrigerated in a tightly sealed container for up to 4 weeks. You may also want to freeze it in small freezer bags to thaw as needed. Grill duck only until medium-rare; if cooked longer it will become tough.

Vegetable Basting Sauce
1/2 cup butter, diced
1/3 cup olive oil
3 tbsp Dijon mustard
1 tbsp grated lemon rind
2 tbsp lemon juice
2 tbsp chopped fresh thyme

In small saucepan, combine butter, oil, mustard, lemon rind and juice and thyme; bring to simmer and set aside.

Benmiller Inn's Barbecue Sauce
2 cups chopped onions
1/2 cup vegetable oil
1/4 cup minced garlic
1 1/2 tbsp ground cumin
1 tsp cayenne pepper
2 cups ketchup
1/2 cup balsamic vinegar
1/2 cup soy sauce

1/3 cup brown sugar
1/4 cup red wine vinegar
1/4 cup Worcestershire sauce
1 tsp Tabasco Sauce

In blender or food processor, purée together onions, oil, garlic, cumin and cayenne; sauté in saucepan over medium-low heat until soft. Add ketchup, balsamic vinegar, soy sauce, brown sugar, red wine vinegar, Worcestershire sauce and Tabasco Sauce; stir until blended. Reduce heat to low and simmer for 4 to 6 hours.

1 bunch asparagus
1 eggplant, cut into large cubes
1 sweet red pepper, coarsely chopped
1 sweet green pepper, coarsely chopped
1 red onion, cut into 8 sections
6 boneless skinless duck breasts, each 6 oz
toasted unsweetened coconut

Cut each asparagus spear in half lengthwise. In bowl, combine asparagus, eggplant, red and green peppers and onion; toss with 1/4 cup of the vegetable basting sauce. Place vegetables in grilling basket over medium-high heat; cook, turning basket occasionally and basting regularly with remaining sauce, for about 10 minutes or until tender.

Meanwhile, place duck breasts on grill; cook, basting regularly with barbecue sauce, for about 5 minutes per side or until medium-rare.

To serve, carefully slice breasts into thin strips and arrange on serving platter in star pattern. Divide grilled vegetables among plates. Sprinkle with toasted coconut. Serves 6.

Chef's wine suggestion — Baco Noir, Henry of Pelham

GRILLED PROVIMI VEAL CHOP WITH A FARCE OF VARIOUS MUSHROOMS, SPINACH AND ASIAGO CHEESE
The Westover Inn
Executive Chef: Michael Hoy

Chef Hoy suggests serving this great-tasting veal dish with rösti potatoes (recipe follows), roasted baby onions and parsley root.

Fanshawe Lake, London

Grilled Provimi Veal Chop

1/4 cup olive oil
4 large shallots, finely minced
2 cups finely minced mixed mushrooms
(portobello, shiitake, oyster, etc.)
1/3 cup cooked, drained chopped fresh or
frozen spinach
4 tsp finely minced garlic
2 tbsp bread crumbs
1/2 cup shredded Asiago cheese
salt and pepper
6 Provimi veal chops, each 8 oz

In skillet, heat oil over medium heat; sauté
shallots until translucent. Add mushrooms,
spinach, garlic and bread crumbs; sauté for 2
minutes. Let cool. Add Asiago cheese. Mix
thoroughly; season with salt and pepper to taste.

Make incision about 3/4 inch long and 1 1/2
inches deep on fat side of veal chop near bone.
Stuff pocket with mushroom mixture and secure
with toothpicks. In skillet heat oil over high
heat, sear veal for about 2 minutes per side.
Place on baking sheet and roast in 375°F oven
for 10 to 12 minutes.

Rösti Potatoes
6 Yukon Gold potatoes, peeled
salt and pepper
4 tsp unsalted butter

In food processor, grate potatoes. Squeeze out
excess water and season with salt and pepper to
taste.

In nonstick skillet over medium-high heat,
melt half of the butter. Layer grated potato in
skillet and pack down to form 1 large pancake;
cook until browned. Place large inverted plate
over pancake. Turn over skillet so that pancake is
transferred to plate. Add remaining butter to
skillet and slide pancake back into skillet; cook
until browned. Place on baking sheet and roast
in 375°F oven for about 10 minutes or until
potatoes are tender. Serve with veal. Serves 6.

Chef's wine suggestion — Cabernet Franc,
Vineland Estates

OSSO BUCO

Trattoria Il Timone
Executive Chef: Michel Fronteddu

This classic entrée is always inviting on a cold winter day. Serve it with your favourite pasta or risotto.

6 centre-cut Provimi veal shanks, 1 inch thick
1 tbsp olive oil
4 ribs celery, coarsely diced
2 Spanish onions, coarsely diced
1 carrot, coarsely diced
6 cloves garlic, thinly sliced
2 cups tomato purée
2 cups rich beef broth or canned beef broth
1 cup heavy red wine
pinch saffron (optional)
pinch rosemary
pinch thyme
6 bay leaves

Place veal in greased roasting pan; brown in 450°F oven for 5 minutes. Turn over and cook for 5 minutes longer. Remove from oven and reduce temperature to 325°F.

In skillet, heat oil over medium heat; sauté celery, onions, carrots and garlic until lightly browned. Pour over veal. Stir in tomato purée, broth, wine, saffron (if using), rosemary, thyme and bay leaves. Cover and roast in 325°F oven for 2 to 2 1/2 hours or until meat falls away from bone. Remove bay leaves.

Place veal on each of 6 warmed plates and spoon sauce over top. Serves 6.

Chef's wine suggestion — Cabernet Sauvignon, Henry of Pelham

PORK TENDERLOIN WITH FOUR PEPPERCORN CRUST AND APPLE CALVADOS JUS

The Elm Hurst Inn
Executive Chef: Darrell Stewart

The slight fruity flavour of the sauce offsets the spiciness of the peppercorns in this delightful entrée. The creamy buttered spinach accents the pork nicely.

3 tbsp coarsely crushed peppercorns (pink, green, black and white)
3 pork tenderloins, each 12 oz (tail ends cut off and trimmed)
1/4 cup clarified butter
1/4 cup Calvados or brandy
1/2 cup apple cider
3/4 cup homemade beef jus lié (or Knorr demi-glaze or jus lié)
1/4 cup butter
1 1/2 bags (10 oz) fresh spinach
3 medium portobello mushrooms, cut into quarters
3 tbsp olive oil
1 clove garlic, minced
salt and pepper

Sprinkle crushed peppercorns over 1 side of each tenderloin; press lightly onto pork.

In ovenproof skillet over medium-high heat, heat clarified butter; sear pork, peppercorn side down. Turn over and roast in 400°F oven for about 15 minutes or until juices run clear when pork is pierced and just a hint of pink remains inside. Remove from skillet and keep warm.

Drain fat from pan. Over high heat, deglaze pan with brandy. Add apple cider and jus lié; reduce by one-third.

In separate large skillet, melt butter; add 2 tbsp water. Add spinach; sauté just until wilted. Set aside.

Toss mushrooms with olive oil and garlic; season with salt and pepper to taste. Transfer to barbecue over medium heat or under broiler; grill on both sides.

Slice each pork tenderloin into about 8 slices. Divide spinach among 6 plates. Fan pork slices over top. Spoon sauce over pork and top with mushrooms. Serves 6.

Chef's wine suggestion — Gewürztraminer, 1996, Vineland Estates

GRILLED ONTARIO PORK TENDERLOIN WITH RIESLING CREAM CORN AND ASPARAGUS CRISPIN APPLE FRITTERS

Hillebrand's Vineyard Café
Executive Chef: Tony de Luca

The colourful and fresh Harvest Riesling cream corn and the fritters are a beautiful combination with the pork tenderloin.

Harvest Riesling Cream Corn

6 ears corn
1 tbsp olive oil
1 shallot, finely diced
1 clove garlic, minced
1/2 sweet red pepper, cut into 1/4-inch pieces
1/2 sweet yellow pepper, cut into 1/4-inch pieces
1/4 cup Hillebrand's Harvest Riesling 1995
1/2 cup 35% cream
salt and pepper

Husk and clean corn. Slice off kernels. In skillet, heat oil over medium-high heat; sauté shallots, garlic, corn and red and yellow peppers for 2 minutes. Add wine and reduce to 1 tablespoon. Blend in cream and salt and pepper to taste. Keep warm.

Asparagus Crispin Apple Fritters

3/4 cups all purpose flour
1/2 cup bread flour
3 tsp baking powder
1 tsp salt
2 large eggs, beaten
2 cups milk
2 tbsp maple syrup
3/4 cup chopped pecans
1/2 Crispin apple, peeled, cored and chopped into 1/4-inch pieces
3 tsp minced fresh gingerroot
1/2 cup peeled chopped (1/2-inch pieces) asparagus
3 cups vegetable oil

In bowl, combine all-purpose and bread flours, baking powder, and salt.
In separate bowl, blend together eggs, milk and maple syrup. Stir in pecans, apple, ginger and asparagus.

Stir apple mixture into flour mixture until blended.
In deep saucepan, heat oil over high heat to 350°F; spoon heaping tablespoon of batter into hot oil and cook until golden brown. Remove with slotted spoon and let drain on paper towel. Repeat with remaining batter. Keep warm.

Pork Tenderloins

2 pork tenderloins, each 1 lb
2 tbsp olive oil
salt, pepper and cayenne pepper

Brush pork with oil. Season with salt, pepper and cayenne to taste. On grill over high heat, cook tenderloins for 8 minutes; turn and grill for about 4 minutes longer or just until hint of pink remains inside. Cut into 1 1/2-inch slices.

To Assemble: Spoon about 1/4 cup of the Harvest Riesling cream corn onto each of 4 warmed plates. Fan 3 slices of pork tenderloin on top of sauce. Arrange 3 fritters attractively around plate. Serves 4.

Chef's tip: The fritter mixture can be made up to 2 hours in advance.

Chef's wine suggestion — Lakeshore Chardonnay, 1995, Hillebrand Estates

Grilled Ontario Pork Tenderloin

69

ROAST LOIN OF WILD BOAR WITH TWICE-BAKED APPLE CALVADOS SOUFFLÉ AND PURPLE ELDERBERRY GAME JUS

Grosvenor's
Owner/Chef: Paul Johnston

This entrée features sliced oven-roasted wild boar topped with a warm apple Calvados soufflé. The purple elderberry game jus is drizzled over the soufflé and around the boar. Chef Johnston serves it with baby turned vegetables and finishes with a thyme garnish. Serve your choice of vegetables alongside the meat.

Roast Wild Boar Loin and Purple Elderberry Game Jus

1 wild boar loin roast, 4 to 5 lb (Wehrmann Farms, Lucknow in Bruce County, Ontario)
1 3/4 cups Cave Spring Cellars Gamay red wine
1 1/2 cups water
1 onion, chopped

Hillebrand Estates Winery

1 stalk celery, chopped
1 carrot, chopped
3 sprigs fresh rosemary
4 cloves garlic
1/2 cup elderberries
1 tbsp unsalted butter
1 tbsp cornstarch

Place roast in roasting pan. Stir in 1 cup of the wine and 3/4 cup of the water. Braise in 500°F oven for 20 minutes. Add onion, celery, carrot, rosemary and garlic; reduce temperature to 375°F and roast for about 2 hours or until medium.

Remove roast from pan and strain braising liquid into saucepan. Deglaze pan with remaining wine and water. Strain into reserved braising liquid. Using ladle, remove fat from jus. Add elderberries and heat over medium-high heat. Whisk in butter. Dissolve cornstarch in 1/2 cup water; add to jus and cook just until thick enough to coat back of spoon.

Twice-Baked Apple Calvados Soufflé

8 Granny Smith apples, peeled and cored
1/3 cup Calvados
pinch cinnamon
12 egg whites
1 tbsp unsalted butter
6 sprigs thyme

In food processor, purée 7 of the apples. Add one-third of the Calvados and the cinnamon.

Beat egg whites until stiff peaks form; fold in apple purée.

Butter 6 3-inch ramekins. Dice remaining apple and divide among ramekins. Pour in soufflé mixture and level off. Slide finger around outside of each ramekin to push mixture away from edge. Bake in 350°F oven for about 10 minutes or until golden brown. Let stand for 10 minutes. Run small knife around edge of each dish. Turn upside down onto each of 6 plates and remove.

Slice boar and arrange slices in centre of each of 6 plates. Reheat soufflé in oven for 1 minute and set on top of meat. Drizzle hot elderberry game jus over and around meat. Garnish each with thyme sprig. Serves 6.

Chef's tip: As long as the boar is grain-fed it can be cooked medium. If it is cooked beyond this point, it starts to become tough.

Chef's wine suggestion — Gamay, Cave Spring Cellars

MEDALLIONS OF LAMB WITH APRICOTS AND PEPPERCORN HONEY GLAZE
The Glenerin Inn
Executive Chef: John Harnett

Chef Harnett suggests a variation using Ontario maple syrup instead of the honey and fresh apricots instead of the dried.

2 1/2 lb boneless loin of lamb
1 cup all-purpose flour
salt and pepper
6 to 8 tbsp (approx) unsalted butter
4 tsp crushed green peppercorns
1 1/2 cups dry white wine
1 1/2 cups liquid honey

12 dried apricots
fresh mint

Cut lamb into 1 1/2-inch-thick slices. Place medallions between 2 pieces of waxed paper; using meat mallet, flatten to uniform thickness. In bowl, season flour with salt and pepper to taste; dredge medallions in flour mixture.

In large skillet, melt 2 tbsp of the butter over medium-high heat; sauté medallions in batches (adding more butter as necessary) until cooked to desired doneness and lightly browned on both sides. Transfer to serving platter, cover with foil and keep warm in oven.

Drain excess butter from skillet; add peppercorns to skillet; sauté for 1 minute. Add wine, honey and apricots; bring to boil and simmer for 15 to 20 minutes or until apricots are tender and sauce is thickened to consistency of syrup. Spoon apricots and sauce over the lamb medallions. Garnish with mint. Serves 6.

Chef's wine suggestion — Baco Noir, VQA, 1996, Henry of Pelham

Glenerin Inn, Mississauga

Niagara-on-the-Lake

STEAK AU POIVRE
Bailey's
Owner/Chef: Ben Merritt

This classic steak has always been on Chef Merritt's menu and probably always will be because some things just shouldn't change.

2 tbsp olive oil
4 striploin steaks, each 8 oz
1/4 cup beef or veal stock
1/4 cup 35% cream
green peppercorn butter (recipe follows)
salt
chopped fresh parsley

Green Peppercorn Butter
1/2 cup butter
2 tbsp brandy
2 tbsp green peppercorns + 1/2 tsp peppercorn
brine
1/2 tsp pepper
pinch salt

Green Peppercorn Butter: In food processor or blender, combine butter, brandy, peppercorns, peppercorn brine, pepper and salt.

In large skillet, heat oil over medium-high heat; sauté steaks until cooked to desired doneness. Keep warm in oven.

Drain any fat from skillet; add stock and cream and reduce by half. Add green peppercorn butter and reduce until sauce is thick enough to coat back of wooden spoon. Season with salt to taste. Spoon sauce over steaks; garnish with parsley. Serves 4.

Chef's wine suggestion — Trius Red, VQA, 1995, Hillebrand Estates

Forks of the Credit River

Prince of Wales Hotel, Niagara-on-the-Lake

GRILLED VENISON CHOP WITH WILTED ARUGULA, RADICCHIO, ENDIVE AND WALNUT BREAD
The Prince of Wales Hotel
Executive Chef: Ralf Bretzigheimer

This creation of Chef Bretzigheimer is truly delicious, with its wonderful gravy for the venison chop, accompanied by the nut-flavoured wilted lettuces.

1 large bunch arugula
2 heads Belgian endive
1 1/2 large heads radicchio
1 cup frozen cranberries
1 cup Merlot
1/2 cup granulated sugar
1 cup glace de viande, or canned beef or veal gravy
salt and pepper
3 medium Yukon Gold potatoes (unpeeled)
4 tbsp olive oil
2 tbsp butter
3 cups walnut bread, cubed (or dark rye bread and 1/4 cup chopped walnuts)
2 tbsp raspberry vinegar
6 venison loin chops, bone in and frenched

Wash and dry arugula, endive and radicchio. Chop into 1/4-inch strips and set aside.

In saucepan over high heat, combine the cranberries, Merlot and sugar. Bring to boil; boil, stirring constantly, until reduced by one-third. Add glace de viande and salt and pepper to taste. Keep warm over low heat.

Scrub potatoes and cut into 1-inch-thick slices. Arrange on small baking sheet and brush with 2 tbsp of the oil. Bake in 300°F oven until tender.

In large skillet, heat butter over medium-high heat; briefly sauté walnut bread. Add arugula, endive, radicchio and raspberry vinegar; cook until greens are slightly wilted.

In separate large skillet, heat remaining oil over high heat; sear venison chops until medium to medium-rare; keep warm. Arrange potatoes on 1 side of each plate, overlapping in fan shape. On other side of each plate, pile greens mixture. Arrange venison, bone up, in centre of plates. Serves 6.

Chef's wine suggestion — Baco Noir, VQA, 1996, Henry of Pelham

PHYLLO PIE
Paradiso
Executive Chef: Michael D. Killip

Chef Killip says that the tomatoes in this classic entrée can either be added fresh or roasted first in a hot oven with a little garlic, balsamic vinegar and salt and pepper.

1 lb feta cheese
1 lb ricotta cheese
milk
pinch nutmeg
salt and pepper
1 pkg (1 lb) phyllo pastry
1/2 lb sweet butter, melted
1 lb Roma tomatoes, sliced
1 lb fresh spinach, washed and dried

Blend together feta and ricotta cheeses. Thin mixture with a little milk. Season with nutmeg and salt and pepper to taste.

Brush 13- x 9-inch baking dish with butter. Place 2 phyllo sheets in dish and brush each with butter. Repeat to make six layers. Spread with one-quarter of the cheese mixture, tomatoes and spinach. Make 6 more layers of phyllo; spread with another one-quarter of the cheese mixture, tomatoes and spinach. Layer twice more. Butter final layer well. Cover with foil and bake in 375°F oven for 40 minutes. Remove foil during last 5 minutes to allow pastry to brown. Serves 6 to 8.

Chef's wine suggestion — Pinot Noir, 1995, Henry of Pelham

CHEESE SOUFFLÉ
Enver's
Owner/Chef: Enver Bismallah

The good thing about this recipe is that most of the ingredients are right in your refrigerator. You can use any assortment of leftover cheeses such as Cheddar and Stilton. Served with a salad and bread, the soufflé makes a nice lunch or light dinner.

2 tbsp butter
2 tbsp cornstarch
1/2 cup milk
1/2 cup 35% cream
1/2 cup assorted grated cheeses
salt and pepper

Niagara River from the Glen

4 egg yolks
5 egg whites

In small saucepan, melt the butter over medium heat; blend in cornstarch until smooth. Add milk, cream and cheeses. Cook until cheese is melted; season with salt and pepper to taste.

Add egg yolks to cheese mixture; stir until smooth. Beat egg whites until stiff peaks form; carefully fold in cheese mixture.

Pour into greased baking dish. Place baking dish in roasting pan; pour enough water into pan to come halfway up sides of baking dish. Bake in 350°F oven for 25 minutes. Serves 4 to 6.

Chef's wine suggestion — Reserve Chardonnay, Cave Spring Cellars

GRILLED VEGETABLE AND TOFU TORTES
The Wildflower Restaurant
Owner/Chef: Wolfgang Sterr

This entrée is very popular at The Wildflower, especially in the late summer and harvest season, *when all the vegetables have the most flavour and local farmers have lots to offer. In the fall, use some butternut squash or even pumpkin.*

1 medium green zucchini
1 medium yellow zucchini
1 medium eggplant
4 Roma tomatoes
1 small red onion
2 sweet red peppers
2 sweet green peppers
1/2 cup extra-virgin olive oil
1/2 cup balsamic vinegar
3 tsp chopped fresh cilantro
2 tsp chopped fresh garlic
salt and pepper
1 block (12.4 oz) extra-firm tofu
6 sheets (each 7 inches square) homemade or purchased pasta
2 cups homemade tomato and herb compote (or jar of tomato sauce enriched by adding two chopped Roma tomatoes)
1/2 cup shredded medium Cheddar cheese
1/2 cup shredded mozzarella cheese

baby greens to serve 6
1 cup of "Wildflowers" Fieldberry Vinaigrette (or homemade or purchased raspberry vinaigrette)

Cut green and yellow zucchini, eggplant, tomatoes and onion into 1/4-inch-thick slices. Cut red and green peppers into 1 1/2-inch-wide strips. Whisk together oil, vinegar, cilantro, garlic and salt and pepper to taste. Add vegetables to oil mixture and marinate for 2 hours. Transfer to barbecue grill over medium-high heat; grill until almost cooked. Remove and set aside.

Cut tofu into thin slices. Blanch pasta sheets until almost cooked.

Brush baking sheet with olive oil. On sheet, layer eggplant slice, 1 tsp tomato compote, zucchini, tofu, tomato, onion and peppers, adding more compote after each layer and finishing with pasta sheet. Sprinkle with Cheddar and mozzarella. Bake in 375°F oven for 5 to 8 minutes or until cheese is melted.

Grilled Vegetable and Tofu Torte

Toss greens in vinaigrette and arrange on 6 plates. Heat remaining tomato compote and top greens with 2 tsp each. Place grilled vegetable pasta torte on compote. Serves 6.

Chef's wine suggestion — Pinot Noir, 1996, Konzelmann

LENTIL AND VEGETABLE TORTES
The Wildflower Restaurant
Owner/Chef: Wolfgang Sterr

This very flavourful and healthy torte can be served with salsa and salad or on focaccia as a sandwich. It also freezes quite well according to Chef Sterr.

2 cups green lentils
1 cup red lentils
2 medium carrots
2 stalks celery
1 cup coarsely chopped turnip
1 small onion
3 tsp chopped mixed fresh herbs (basil, parsley, thyme)
1 tsp minced garlic
1 large egg
1 to 3 cups (approx) oatmeal
pinch each salt, pepper and chili flakes
1 tbsp olive oil

In large bowl, cover green and red lentils with water and soak overnight.

In saucepan over medium-low heat, simmer lentils in water until soft. Cool under cold running water; drain well.

In food processor, chop carrots, celery, turnip and onion until fine. Combine lentils, chopped vegetables, herbs and garlic. Blend in egg and 1 cup of the oatmeal. Let stand for 5 minutes to absorb liquid. Sprinkle up to 2 more cups of the oatmeal into the mixture a little at a time until thick and holds together. Season with salt, pepper and chili flakes. Shape mixture into patties. In nonstick skillet, heat oil over medium heat; fry patties until golden brown. Serves 6.

Chef's wine suggestion — Semi-dry Riesling, Vineland Estates

Creamy Lemon Delight with Strawberries

DESSERTS

Dessert! After a family meal, a dessert can be simple: sliced fruit or cookies. But a dinner party calls for something special — an elegant, sweet conclusion to the meal. It's the last thing your guests will have at your home, and you will want them to leave with a wonderful sweet taste in their mouths. A dessert had better be sufficiently decadent and delicious to be worth the calories.

These recipes surely are. Included in this section are innovative ways to serve fresh fruit such as Raspberries with Mango Sorbet from Rundles, or Niagara Fruit Cobbler from On the Twenty. There are wonderfully rich selections such as Creamy Lemon Delight with Cointreau Marinated Strawberries from The Little Inn of Bayfield and Crème Brûlée with Toffeed Strawberries from The Church Restaurant.

For those of you with a sweet tooth, this selection of desserts is sure to satisfy.

Lakewinds, Niagara-on-the-Lake

STRAWBERRY MOUSSE WITH STRAWBERRY SAUCE
Beild House Country Inn
Owner/Chef: Bill Barclay

We all love strawberries when they're in season and this heavenly dessert is a great way to enjoy them.

Strawberry Sauce
2 cups sliced fresh or frozen strawberries
2 cups granulated sugar
juice of 1 lemon

In saucepan, combine strawberries, sugar and lemon juice; bring to simmer and cook for 10 minutes. Let cool. Pressing strawberries through sieve or food mill, strain into bowl. Set aside 2 cups for mousse; cover and refrigerate remaining sauce.

Strawberry Mousse
1 1/2 cups 35% cream
juice of 1 lemon
2 cups Strawberry Sauce (recipe above)
1 1/2 envelopes gelatin
3 tbsp cold water

Beat cream until stiff peaks form; set aside. Stir lemon juice into strawberry sauce; set aside.

In heatproof bowl, sprinkle gelatin over cold water; let soften for 5 minutes. Place bowl over saucepan of simmering water and let stand until liquefied. Working quickly, whisk gelatin into strawberry sauce mixture. Fold in whipped cream. Spoon mousse into individual serving dishes or large bowl and refrigerate for at least 6 hours or overnight. Serve with reserved strawberry sauce. Serves 12.

Chef's wine suggestion — Framboise D'Or, Southbrook

LEMON AND MASCARPONE MOUSSE IN PHYLLO
Wellington Court
Executive Chef: Erik Peacock

The contrasting textures of the mousse with the crispness of the phyllo cup make a heavenly dessert.

3/4 cup unsalted butter
1 cup granulated sugar
1/3 cup lemon juice

4 eggs
1 cup 35% cream
1/4 cup mascarpone cheese
6 sheets phyllo pastry
icing sugar

In medium saucepan over low heat, melt 1/2 cup of the butter. Stir in sugar and lemon juice; cook, stirring frequently and without boiling, until sugar is dissolved. Remove from heat.

Whisk eggs. Add lemon mixture and stir until well blended and smooth. Return to saucepan and cook over medium heat, stirring constantly, for about 15 minutes or until thick enough to coat back of wooden spoon.

Pass mixture through sieve into stainless steel or glass bowl. Prepare ice water bath in second bowl. Place bowl of lemon custard in ice water bath and let cool completely.

Meanwhile, whisk 3 tbsp of the cream with mascarpone cheese. In separate bowl, whip remaining cream and set aside in refrigerator. Fold mascarpone cheese into chilled custard until incorporated. Fold in whipped cream. Refrigerate for at least 2 hours or overnight.

Phyllo Pastry Cups: Melt remaining butter. Cut 3 sheets phyllo pastry evenly into 4 to make 12 rectangles. Cover with damp towel to prevent drying out.

Arrange 4 single sheets of phyllo on work surface and brush each with butter. Top each with 2 more sheets, brushing each layer with butter. Place in muffin cups or other cup form. Repeat to make 4 more cups. Bake in 350°F oven for 6 minutes or until golden brown. Sprinkle with icing sugar. (Can be stored, uncovered, at room temperature for up to 1 day.) Fill phyllo cups with lemon mascarpone mousse. Serves 8.

Chef's tip: Serve phyllo cups alone or with fruit purée for colour on the plate.

Chef's wine suggestion — Late Harvest Riesling, Château des Charmes

Lemon and Mascarpone Mousse in Phyllo

Stratford

CHOCOLATE MOUSSE WITH ARMAGNAC
Enver's
Owner/Chef: Enver Bismallah

This is so rich, velvety and delicious that it's hard to believe it's so easy to make.

4 eggs, separated
6 oz (or squares) semisweet chocolate
2 tbsp Armagnac
2/3 cup 35% cream

In bowl, beat egg whites until stiff peaks form. In saucepan over low heat, melt chocolate; blend into egg yolks. Add Armagnac. Fold in egg whites.
   Beat cream until stiff peaks form; fold into chocolate mixture. Pour into serving dishes and refrigerate until serving. Serves 6.

Chef's wine suggestion — Indian Summer, Cave Spring Cellars

WHITE CHOCOLATE MOUSSE TORTE
Rinderlin's
Executive Chef: Jeff Pitchot

This velvety smooth torte features the contrasting flavours of chocolate and raspberry. If you are short on time, you can purchase a sponge cake.

Vanilla Sponge Cake
5 eggs
1 egg yolk
1 cup granulated sugar
2 drops lemon juice
1 cup all-purpose flour, sifted
1/2 tbsp vanilla powder

Beat together eggs, egg yolk, sugar and lemon juice until frothy. Fold in flour and vanilla powder. Pour into 9-inch springform pan. Bake in 450°F oven for 10 minutes. Reduce temperature to 350°F and bake for 25 minutes longer. Let cool; remove from pan.

White Chocolate Mousse
15 oz white chocolate, chopped
4 egg yolks

Spanish aerocar over the Niagara River Whirlpool

1 1/2 cups 35% cream
5 egg whites
1 1/2 tbsp granulated sugar

In top of double boiler set over hot (not boiling) water, melt white chocolate, stirring, until smooth. Beat egg yolks until smooth; blend into chocolate. Set aside.

Beat cream until stiff peaks form. Beat egg whites with sugar until stiff peaks form; fold into chocolate mixture. Fold in whipped cream. Cover and set aside in refrigerator.

Liqueur-Enhanced Simple Syrup
1/3 cup granulated sugar
1/3 cup water
2 tbsp Amaretto
2 tbsp Kahlúa

In saucepan, bring sugar and water to boil; cook, stirring, until sugar is dissolved. Remove from heat and let cool in refrigerator. Stir in Amaretto and Kahlúa.

Raspberry Sauce
1 pkg (10 oz) frozen raspberries
5 tbsp granulated sugar

1 tbsp cornstarch
1/2 cup seedless raspberry jam

Thaw raspberries, reserving juice. In saucepan, bring raspberries and sugar to a boil. Dissolve cornstarch in 2 tbsp water; stir into raspberry mixture and simmer, stirring, for 1 to 2 minutes. Purée in food processor and strain. Cover and set aside in refrigerator.

To Assemble: Slice sponge cake horizontally into 3 equal layers. Place 1 layer in bottom of 9-inch springform pan. Moisten each layer of sponge cake with liqueur-enhanced simple syrup. Spread 1/4 cup seedless raspberry jam on each of bottom and middle layers. Spread one-quarter of the white chocolate mousse on each of bottom and middle layers and one-quarter on top.

Cover and refrigerate torte and remaining mousse for at least 6 hours or overnight. Remove pan; spread reserved mousse on sides of torte. Serve with raspberry sauce. Serves 12 to 14.

Chef's tip: Decorate with chocolate shavings and fresh berries.

Chef's wine suggestion — Late Harvest Vidal, Vineland Estates

HAZELNUT CAPPUCCINO TORTE
Kettle Creek Inn
Executive Chef: Frank Hubert

Hazelnut, chocolate and coffee! What a winning combination in this heavenly, creamy dessert.

3/4 cup toasted hazelnuts
5 1/2 oz bittersweet chocolate
2 tsp orange rind
1 tsp lemon rind
6 large eggs, separated
3/4 cup granulated sugar
8 oz mascarpone cheese
3/4 cup 35% cream
1/8 cup coffee liqueur
1/8 cup Frangelico
1 tbsp espresso granules
freshly ground nutmeg

In food processor, chop hazelnuts, chocolate and orange and lemon rind until finely ground. Set aside.

Beat egg yolks with 1/4 cup of the sugar for 5 minutes or until creamy consistency. Fold into hazelnut mixture.

In separate bowl, beat egg whites until frothy. Gradually beat in another 1/4 cup of the sugar until soft peaks form. Beat until stiff peaks form; fold into hazelnut mixture. Spread in greased floured 8-inch springform pan; bake in 350°F oven for 30 minutes. Let cool; unmould.

In bowl, combine mascarpone cheese, cream, remaining sugar, coffee liqueur and Frangelico; beat until smooth and stiff; spread over cake. Just before serving sprinkle with the espresso granules and nutmeg. Serves 10 to 12.

Chef's wine suggestion — Cabernet Franc, VQA, Pelee Island

CLAFOUTIS
The Old Prune Restaurant
Executive Chef: Bryan Steele

This is one of the most popular desserts on The Old Prune's summer menu. It's a soufflé-like baked dish that combines the contrasting elements of hot and cold, sour and sweet. Quark is a low-fat cheese readily available in most supermarkets.

The Little Inn of Bayfield

2 cups Quark, drained and pressed through sieve
1 1/2 tbsp unsalted butter, softened
2 cups icing sugar
4 egg yolks
1/4 cup 35% cream
rind and juice of 1/2 lemon
1/4 cup cornstarch, sifted
4 egg whites
2 tbsp granulated sugar
1 cup fresh berries (raspberries, blackberries, wild blueberries) or pitted cherries
ice cream

In bowl, beat Quark and butter until light and fluffy. Add icing sugar and continue beating until very light. Beat in egg yolks, 1 at a time. Beat in cream, lemon rind and juice and cornstarch just until combined.

Beat egg whites until soft peaks form; fold into Quark mixture. Grease an 8- x 12-inch glass baking dish or individual 4-inch ramekins. Sprinkle lightly with granulated sugar. Spoon in Quark mixture to come two-thirds of the way up dish. Arrange berries on top. Bake in 450°F oven for 25 to 30 minutes or until tester inserted in centre comes out clean. If baking in individual ramekins, bake for 12 to 15 minutes. Serve warm with scoop of ice cream on top. Serves 6 to 8.

Chef's wine suggestion — Winter Wine, 1995, Marynissen Estates

CREAMY LEMON DELIGHT WITH COINTREAU-MARINATED STRAWBERRIES
The Little Inn of Bayfield
Executive Chef: Jamie Stearns

This dessert is so simple to prepare, yet the presentation and flavour are out of this world.

3 1/3 cups 35% cream
1 cup granulated sugar + 2 tbsp
1/2 tbsp gelatin
rind of 3 lemons
juice of 4 lemons
1/2 cup Cointreau
36 whole strawberries, washed, dried and stems removed (kept whole)
6 mint bouquets

In saucepan over medium heat, combine cream, 1 cup of the sugar and gelatin; cook without boiling, until gelatin is dissolved. Whisk rind and juice of 3 lemons into warm cream mixture. Pour into 6 martini or dessert glasses; refrigerate for about 4 hours or until set.

Stir together Cointreau, juice of remaining lemon and remaining 2 tbsp sugar. Pour over strawberries. Let marinate until serving.

To serve, place 6 strawberries, pointed end up, on top of set cream. Pour Cointreau marinade over top. Garnish with mint leaves. Serves 6.

Chef's wine suggestion — Icewine Wild Yeasts VQA, 1995, Château des Charmes

NIAGARA FRUIT COBBLER
On The Twenty Restaurant & Wine Bar
Vintner's Inn
Executive Chef: Michael Olson

I don't think you can beat an old-fashioned cobbler for dessert. Serve it with ice cream or whipped cream.

Topping
1 1/2 cups all-purpose flour
1/2 cup granulated sugar
1/4 cup cornmeal
1 tsp baking powder
pinch salt
1/4 cup cold unsalted butter
1/2 to 2/3 cup (approx) milk
1 tsp vanilla

Filling
3 to 4 medium pears, peeled and sliced
4 Italian prune plums, pitted and quartered
1/2 cup granulated sugar
1 tsp cinnamon

Topping: In bowl, combine flour, sugar, cornmeal, baking powder and salt. Cut in butter until mixture resembles coarse meal. Gradually add 1/2 cup milk, stirring constantly and adding remaining milk if necessary to make consistency that is thicker than cake batter but thinner than cookie dough. Stir in vanilla.

Filling: Toss together pears, plums, sugar and cinnamon; spoon into baking dish. Cover with topping, leaving a little space for topping to expand. Bake in 350°F oven for 40 to 50 minutes. Serves 6 to 8.

Chef's wine suggestion — Indian Summer Riesling, Cave Spring Cellars

Kayaking on the Saugeen River, Southampton

Crème Brûlée with Toffeed Strawberries

CRÈME BRÛLÉE WITH TOFFEED STRAWBERRIES

The Church Restaurant
Owner/Chef: Sheldon Russell

This beautifully rich and creamy dessert continues to be a favourite.

Crème Brûlée

1 vanilla bean, split and seeds scraped out
1/2 cup milk + 2 tbsp
1 3/4 cups 35% cream
6 1/2 tbsp superfine sugar
9 egg yolks

Caramel Top for Crème Brûlée

6 tbsp superfine sugar

Mix vanilla seeds with 2 tbsp milk to separate. In bowl, mix together cream, 1/2 cup of the milk, sugar, egg yolks, vanilla pod and seeds. Let stand for 1 hour for flavours to infuse; remove pods.

Pour mixture into 6 2-inch ramekins. Set ramekins in roasting pan and fill pan with enough hot water to come two-thirds of the way up sides of ramekins. Cover pan with foil and bake in 250°F oven for about 1 hour or until set, checking periodically to make sure water is not simmering (if it is, reduce heat to 200°F). Remove ramekins from pan and let cool.

Caramel Top for Crème Brûlée: Place plain round pastry cutter about 1/4 inch larger than ramekins on lightly oiled nonstick baking sheet; sprinkle with 1 tbsp of the sugar to make thin layer the shape of cutter. Remove cutter, being careful to keep shape intact. Repeat to make 5 more sugar shapes.

Bake in 400°F oven for about 10 minutes or until sugar caramelizes to golden brown, being careful not to burn. Let cool. Gently remove from tray with palette knife.

Toffeed Strawberries

2 1/4 cups granulated sugar
1/4 cup glucose
12 large strawberries

Pour sugar into saucepan and slowly pour water into centre of sugar, adding just enough to cover.

Bring to boil and skim off white foam. Add glucose and cook, without stirring, over high heat to 305°F on candy thermometer. Remove from heat at about 311°F.

Insert toothpick in each strawberry; holding toothpick, dip each in sugar mixture. Place on a lightly greased nonstick baking sheet or piece of parchment paper.

To Serve: Remove brûlées from ramekins up to 1 hour prior to serving by running knife around edge of ramekin, inverting onto centre of plate and shaking until brûlée releases. Place caramel disc on top. Serve with toffeed strawberries alongside. Serves 6.

Chef's tip: Chef Russell pours crème anglaise around the brûlée and makes a design in it using strawberry sauce. He then places the strawberries along 1 side of the sauce.

Chef's wine suggestion — S.L.H. Vidal, VQA, Henry of Pelham

Goderich

Jakobstettle House

BAKEWELL TART
Bailey's
Owner/Chef: Ben Merritt

This is a traditional northern England favourite.

Pastry
1/4 cup unsalted butter
1 2/3 cups all purpose flour
1 egg
2/3 cup granulated sugar

Filling
1/2 cup unsalted butter
2/3 cup granulated sugar
2 eggs
2/3 cup ground almonds
1/3 cup (heaping) all purpose flour
1/2 cup (approx) raspberry jam
icing sugar

Pastry: In food processor, cut butter into flour until fine. In bowl, beat egg with sugar until well blended. Add to flour mixture and blend thoroughly. Let stand in refrigerator for 20 minutes.

Filling: Meanwhile, cream butter with sugar. Blend in eggs, 1 at a time. Fold in the almonds and flour.

Roll out pastry and place in 9-inch pie plate. Line bottom of pastry with raspberry jam. Spoon filling evenly over top. Bake in 325°F oven for 25 to 30 minutes. Dust with icing sugar during last 3 or 4 minutes of baking. Serve warm. Serves 8 to 10.

Chef's wine suggestion — Winter Pear, Walters Estates

Brandy and Vanilla Custard Cake

BRANDY AND VANILLA CUSTARD CAKE ON THREE-BERRY COMPOTE

The Westover Inn
Executive Chef: Michael Hoy

The contrasting colours and flavours are wonderful in this custard cake. It has a light, sweet-tart flavour. Chef Hoy says that preserved fruit and its liquid also goes well with this dessert, as long as it isn't too sweet.

Custard
1 1/2 cups 35% cream
1 cup milk
2/3 cup granulated sugar
1/2 vanilla bean, split and seeds scraped out
9 egg yolks, lightly beaten
1/4 cup brandy
1 tsp vanilla extract

In saucepan, scald cream and milk along with sugar and vanilla bean and seeds. Let cool. Whisk in yolks. Add brandy and vanilla extract. Strain into 7-inch springform pan lined with plastic wrap. Let stand for 5 minutes to let bubbles escape.

Place in large roasting pan; pour enough water into roasting pan to come halfway up side of springform pan. Cover springform pan with foil. Bake in 325°F oven for about 30 minutes or until custard just sets. (Baking time will vary depending on temperature of mixture when it goes in the oven. Watch carefully, as overbaked custard will turn grainy.) Remove springform pan from water bath; let cool. Cover with plastic wrap and refrigerate until well chilled.

Cake
3 egg whites
1/4 cup granulated sugar + 1 tbsp
1/2 tsp lemon juice
1/2 tsp vanilla extract
1/4 cup sifted cake-and-pastry flour
pinch salt
brandy

Beat egg whites until soft peaks form; beat in 1/4 cup of the sugar. Add lemon juice and vanilla and continue beating. Sift together flour, remaining 1 tbsp sugar and salt. Sift half of the mixture over egg whites and gently fold in with whisk; sift remaining mixture and gently fold in.

Scrape into 7-inch springform pan and bake in 350°F oven for 20 to 25 minutes or until golden brown and top springs back when touched. Place upside down on rack; let cool completely.

Three-Berry Compote
1 cup each frozen strawberries, raspberries and blueberries
1/2 cup granulated sugar
1/2 cup apple juice
juice of 1 lemon

In heavy saucepan over low heat, combine berries, sugar, apple juice and lemon juice. Heat gently just until liquid is hot and berries are thawed. Refrigerate.

To Assemble: Run knife around cake and gently remove from pan. Trim edge to make even.

Gently remove custard from springform pan; remove plastic wrap from sides only. Brush cake with brandy and place over custard. Invert serving platter over cake and turn cake upside down to transfer to plate, custard side up. Remove bottom of springform pan. Trim custard so that edges are flush with cake. Refrigerate.

Slice just before serving. Spoon compote onto plates. Top with cake slice. Serves 10 to 12.

Chef's wine suggestion — Framboise D'Or, Southbrook

APPLE RAISIN CAKE WITH HOMEMADE MAPLE WALNUT ICE CREAM

Keystone Alley Café
Owner/Chef: Sheldon Russell

Chef Russell also serves this cake with a fudge sauce made by simmering a can of condensed milk in a saucepan of water (enough to cover the can) for 2 hours. Remove can and allow to completely cool before opening. When you open it, there is an instant fudge sauce. If it's too thick, add a little water.

Cake

1 cup pecan halves
3/4 cup raisins
1/4 cup bourbon
1 cup sifted cake-and-pastry flour
1 cup all-purpose flour
1 1/2 tsp baking soda
1/2 tsp salt
1/2 tsp nutmeg
1/2 tsp cinnamon
1/4 tsp ground cloves
1/8 tsp mace
2 cups granulated sugar
1 cup vegetable oil
2 large eggs
6 large unpeeled Granny Smith apples, cored and cut into 1/4-inch cubes

Toast pecans and chop coarsely. In bowl, combine pecans, raisins and bourbon; cover and marinate for at least 2 hours.

Sift together cake-and-pastry flour, all-purpose flour and baking soda. Stir in salt, nutmeg, cinnamon, cloves and mace. In separate bowl, beat sugar with oil until well blended. Beat in eggs, 1 at a time. Fold in dry ingredients. Add pecan mixture; mix until combined. Stir in diced apples and pour into greased 10-inch round cake pan. Bake in 325°F oven for 1 1/2 hours or until tester inserted in centre comes out clean and dry. Let cool. Serve with maple walnut ice cream. Serves 10 to 12.

Maple Walnut Ice Cream

7 egg yolks (medium eggs)
1 cup dark maple syrup
2 cups 35% cream, lightly whipped
1/2 cup chopped walnuts

Beat egg yolks lightly.

In saucepan, bring maple syrup to boil; continuing to beat, pour over egg yolks. Beat for 15 to 20 minutes or until cooled. Fold in cream.

Freeze in ice cream machine according to manufacturer's directions, adding walnuts when nearly set; transfer to freezer until frozen. (If using a bowl or mould, add walnuts along with cream. Serve with apple raisin cake.

Chef's wine suggestion — Twenty Valley Vidal Icewine, Cave Spring Cellars

BREAD PUDDING WITH CARAMEL SAUCE
Devlin's Country Bistro
Owner/Chef: Chris Devlin

This delectable pudding can be made a day ahead and gently reheated before serving. Chef Devlin suggests garnishing with fresh raspberries.

Pudding

12 slices crustless bread
1 cup raisins
7 eggs
1 1/2 cups granulated sugar
1/4 tsp vanilla
5 cups 18% cream
1 tsp cinnamon

Grease 13- x 9-inch glass baking dish. Place bread in bottom; sprinkle evenly with raisins.

In bowl, whisk together eggs, sugar and vanilla. In saucepan, bring cream to simmer and stir into egg mixture. Pour over raisins and pat down any loose bread ends. Sprinkle with cinnamon.

Place baking dish in shallow roasting pan; pour in enough water to come halfway up side of dish. Bake in 350°F oven for about 1 hour or until set.

Caramel Sauce

2 tbsp unsalted butter
4 tbsp granulated sugar
2 cups 35% cream, warmed
1 tbsp cornstarch

In heavy saucepan, heat butter and sugar until butter is melted. Pour in warmed cream. Bring to boil. Dissolve cornstarch in 2 tbsp water; stir into pan and cook, stirring, until thickened slightly. Spoon over bread pudding. Serves 8.

Chef's wine suggestion — Icewine, Henry of Pelham

Lake Huron sunset, Southampton

RIESLING-MARINATED BERRIES WITH BREAD AND BUTTER PUDDING
Queen's Landing Inn & Conference Resort
Pastry Chef: Catherine O'Donnell

Frozen berries work as well as fresh for this recipe according to Chef O'Donnell. The amount of berries may be varied depending on the consistency of sauce you desire.

Riesling-Marinated Berries
1/2 bottle Riesling wine
1 1/4 cups icing sugar
1 cup lemon juice
1/3 cup arrowroot or cornstarch
1/2 cup water

1 cup each fresh or frozen blueberries, raspberries and strawberries

In saucepan over medium-high heat, bring wine, sugar and lemon juice to a boil. Dissolve arrowroot in water and blend thoroughly; whisk into wine mixture.

Remove from heat and stir in blueberries. Let cool. Stir in raspberries and strawberries.

Cinnamon Sugar
1 tbsp granulated sugar
1/4 tsp cinnamon

Combine sugar with cinnamon. Set aside.

Bread and Butter Pudding
10 whole eggs
1 cup granulated sugar
1/2 tsp nutmeg
1/2 tsp cinnamon
6 1/4 cups milk
1 cup raisins or apples or cranberries
10 croissants (or 11 slices of bread with crust and 4 tbsp butter)

Whisk eggs with sugar until smooth. Whisk in nutmeg and cinnamon. Stir in milk and strain into bowl. Stir in raisins. Soak bread in milk mixture for 3 to 5 minutes.

Transfer soaked bread to ovenproof casserole. Pour remaining milk mixture over bread. Dust with cinnamon sugar. Place casserole in roasting pan; pour enough water into pan to come one-quarter of the way up side of casserole. Bake in 350°F oven for 45 minutes.

Spoon bread and butter pudding onto each of 8 plates and spoon Riesling-marinated berries on top. Serves 8.

Chef's wine suggestion — Indian Summer Riesling, Cave Spring Cellars

Niagara-on-the-Lake

RASPBERRIES WITH MANGO SORBET
Rundles
Executive Chef: Neil Baxter

This is a delightfully light, colourful dessert full of fresh fruit flavour.

3 pints raspberries
mint leaves

Mango Sorbet
3 ripe mangoes (to yield 4 cups pulp)
1 1/2 cups fruity white wine
1 cup simple syrup (see chef's tip)
juice of 1 lemon

Peel mangoes. Remove flesh from stone and purée in food processor or blender until smooth. Add wine, syrup and lemon juice; blend for 5 seconds. Spoon into ice cream maker and freeze according to manufacturer's instructions.

Raspberry Marinade
1 cup freshly squeezed orange juice
1/2 cup fruity white wine
2 tbsp granulated sugar
juice of 1/2 lemon
6 mint leaves

In bowl, stir together orange juice, wine, sugar, lemon juice and mint leaves until sugar is dissolved. Stir in raspberries and let stand for 1 hour.

Carefully spoon raspberries into individual serving glasses and spoon in enough of the liquid to come two-thirds of the way up berries. Top with scoop of sorbet and garnish with mint leaves. Serves 6.

Chef's tip: To make simple syrup, bring 1/2 cup granulated sugar and 1/2 cup water to boil briefly; let cool. The sorbet base can be made several days ahead and stored in refrigerator. Freeze sorbet several hours ahead of time, but not too long, as ice crystals build up and sorbet will not be as smooth.

Chef's wine suggestion — Framboise D'Or, Southbrook

THYME ICE CREAM
The Other Brother's
Chef: Tim Halley

The essence of this ice cream is in its subtle but unusually distinct flavour. According to Chef Halley, the delicate infusing of the thyme into the cream is the important step to achieve a fabulous result.

2 cups 35% cream
1/2 cup 10% cream
1/2 bunch fresh thyme
6 large egg yolks
1/2 cup granulated sugar
juice of 2 lemons

In saucepan, stir together 35% cream, 10% cream and thyme; bring to boil. Remove from heat and let steep for about 30 minutes, tasting periodically to monitor strength of infusion.
Strain through fine sieve and discard thyme.

Countryside near Caledon

Return cream to saucepan and bring to boil again. Let cool slightly.

Lightly beat egg yolks with sugar. Gradually add cream mixture, whisking constantly. Return to medium heat and cook gently until thick enough to coat back of spoon. Whisk in lemon juice and pass through fine sieve again. Let cool for 20 to 30 minutes.

Freeze in ice cream machine following manufacturer's instructions. Transfer to freezer for at least 4 hours before serving. Serves 6.

Chef's tip: During steeping, the flavouring can become overpowering depending on the size, strength and variety of thyme. Taste periodically to monitor. Taste should be subtle but recognizable.

Chef's wine suggestion — Icewine, 1996, Trius, Hillebrand Estates

HILLEBRAND ESTATE'S TRIUS ICEWINE TRUFFLES
Hillebrand's Vineyard Café
Executive Chef: Tony de Luca

These truffles surprise with a small burst of icewine when you bite into them.

1 lb semisweet chocolate, chopped
1/4 cup 35% cream
1/4 vanilla bean
2 1/2 tbsp unsalted sweet butter, cut in bits
Hillebrand Estate's Trius Icewine
unsweetened cocoa powder or icing sugar

Place chopped chocolate in stainless steel or glass bowl. In small saucepan over high heat, scald cream and vanilla bean. Remove vanilla bean. Immediately pour cream over chocolate; stir gently until chocolate is melted. Stir in butter in small pieces until melted. Let chocolate cool, cover and refrigerate overnight.

Form balls by rolling about 1 tbsp of the mixture in palm of hand. Place on baking sheet, cover and refrigerate for 45 minutes.

Using index finger, form hollow in each truffle. Using syringe, inject hollow with small amount of icewine. Pinch truffle closed. Cover and refrigerate for 2 hours. Dust with cocoa powder. Makes 35 - 40 truffles.

Chef's wine suggestion — Trius Icewine, 1996, Hillebrand Estates

OATMEAL CHOCOLATE CHIP COOKIES
Jakobstettel Guest House
Owner/Chef: Ella Brubacher

These yummy cookies are one of the favourites of Jakobstettel guests

1 cup margarine
1 cup granulated sugar
1 cup brown sugar
2 eggs
1 tsp salt
1 tsp baking soda
1 1/2 cups all-purpose flour
3 cups large-flake oatmeal
1 cup chocolate chips

In bowl, cream the margarine until light.

Gradually beat in the granulated and brown sugars. Add the eggs and 2 tablespoons water. In separate bowl, combine salt, baking soda, flour. Stir into margarine mixture until blended. Stir in oatmeal and chocolate chips. Let stand for 15 minutes.

Using about 1 tablespoon per cookie, drop batter onto greased cookie sheet, flatten slightly. Bake in 350°F for 10 to 12 minutes. Let cool on racks. Makes approximately 48 cookies

Decadent French Toast

BREADS & BREAKFAST FOODS

There is nothing like the aroma of freshly baked bread to bring the whole family into the kitchen.

The Brown, and Muesli Breads from Village Harvest or the Smoked Bacon Corn Bread with Root Cellar Vegetable Slather from The Pillar and Post Inn are delicious, savory, comfort breads — great served on their own or with a soup, stew, or pot of beans. The Sunrise or Scrumptious Egg Casseroles from the Stone Maiden Inn are quick and easy to prepare and would make a special breakfast for family and friends. The Decadent French Toast from the Stone Maiden Inn or Scones with Clotted Cream from Lakewinds Country Manor would make lovely brunch or special occasion breakfasts on Christmas morning or Mother's or Father's Day.

Stone Maiden Inn, Stratford

SCONES WITH NIAGARA-ON-THE-LAKE CLOTTED CREAM
Lakewinds
Owner/Chef: Jane Locke

While Devon cream is available at some specialty shops, it is often costly. This Canadian adaptation is very good. Serve the scones either fresh from the oven or at room temperature with the clotted cream and your favourite jam.

Clotted Cream
1/3 cup milk
1 tsp rose water or vanilla
2 blades mace (or 1/4 tsp ground)
1 egg, beaten
1 1/4 cups 35% cream

In saucepan over low heat, simmer milk, rose water and mace for 5 minutes. Strain milk mixture into beaten egg, then strain whole mixture into cream. Pour into top of double boiler set over simmering water; bring to 165°F. Pour into dish; let cool, cover and refrigerate undisturbed for 24 hours.

Scones
2 cups all-purpose flour
1 tsp cream of tartar
1/2 tsp baking soda
pinch salt
3 tbsp margarine
4 tbsp (approx) milk

In large bowl, sift together flour, cream of tartar, baking soda and salt. Cut margarine into small pieces and rub into flour with fingertips. Stir 4 tbsp of milk with 4 tbsp of water; pour into flour mixture, mixing with round-bladed knife to make a soft, manageable dough.

Knead dough quickly on lightly floured surface to remove all cracks. Roll dough out to 1/2-inch thickness; cut out 2-inch rounds using plain or fluted pastry cutter. Knead trimmings together, roll out and cut out more scones. Transfer to heated, ungreased baking sheet; brush with milk. Bake near top of 450°F oven for about 10 minutes until well risen and light golden. Serve with clotted cream. Makes 10 to 12 scones.

DECADENT FRENCH TOAST
Stone Maiden Inn
Owner/Chef: Barb Woodward

The name of this dish says it all! It makes a lovely Christmas morning breakfast or brunch. According to innkeepers Barb and Len Woodward, you can substitute almost any fruit for the bananas, including small blueberries or peaches. Raisin, egg and homemade breads are also ideal. Prepare the dish the night before, ready to bake in the morning.

2 tbsp corn syrup (preferably dark)
1 cup brown sugar
5 tbsp margarine or butter
16 (approx) slices whole wheat bread, crusts removed
3 or 4 ripe bananas
5 large eggs
1 1/2 cups milk
1 tsp vanilla
1 tbsp cinnamon
1/2 cup sour cream
1 1/2 cups fresh strawberries, hulled (or 1 pkg. 10 oz, frozen unsweetened berries, partially thawed)

In heavy saucepan, combine corn syrup, brown sugar and margarine; cook, stirring constantly, until bubbly.

Pour corn syrup mixture into greased 13- x 9-inch glass baking dish. Nestle half of the bread slices into syrup, trimming to fit corners and edges. Slice bananas and spread over bread. Cover with remaining bread.

Whisk together eggs, milk and vanilla; pour over bread, coating well. Sprinkle with cinnamon. (Can be covered with plastic wrap and refrigerated overnight.)

Bake in 350°F oven for 45 minutes. To serve, loosen edges of bread from dish with knife. Invert serving platter on top and quickly turn baking dish upside down so French toast transfers to platter, caramel side up. Top each serving with 1 tbsp of sour cream and some of the berries. Serves 10 to 12.

SUNRISE CASSEROLE
Stone Maiden Inn
Owner/Chef: Barb Woodward

This variation on the popular morning scramble is simple and quick to prepare and tastes great.

1 cup diced bacon or ham
12 large eggs
1 tbsp milk
1 tbsp margarine or butter
1 cup sour cream
1 cup shredded Cheddar cheese or mixture of shredded cheeses

In skillet, fry bacon. Whisk eggs with milk. In separate skillet heat margarine over medium-high heat, scramble eggs just until soft.

Spread egg mixture in greased 13- x 9-inch glass baking dish. Spread sour cream over top. Sprinkle with bacon and top with cheese. Bake in 350°F oven for 20 minutes. Serves 6 to 8.

Idlewyld Inn, London

Scrumptious Egg Casserole

SCRUMPTIOUS EGG CASSEROLE
Stone Maiden Inn
Owner/Chef: Barb Woodward

This scrumptious egg casserole can be made the night before and popped into the oven in the morning. Innkeepers Barb and Len Woodward use Cheddar cheese but you can use other kinds.

1 1/2 lb shredded Cheddar cheese
1/4 cup butter or margarine
1 can (8 oz) mushrooms, chopped or sliced
1/2 medium onion, chopped
1 cup cubed ham (or crisp bacon)
8 eggs
1 3/4 cups milk
1/2 cup all-purpose flour
1 tsp dried parsley
1 tsp salt

Spread half of the cheese in greased 13- x 9-inch glass baking dish. In saucepan, heat butter over medium heat; sauté mushrooms and onions until tender. Let cool. Spread mushroom mixture over cheese. Top with ham and remaining cheese.

Whisk together eggs, milk, flour, parsley and salt; pour over cheese. Bake in 375°F oven for 60 minutes. Serves 10 to 12.

COUNTRY APPLE AND APRICOT MUFFINS
Queen's Landing Inn & Conference Resort
Pastry Chef: Catherine O'Donnell

Chef O'Donnell recommends Mutsu or Northern Spy apples for these delightful muffins, but any kind will do. She also suggests refrigerating the batter for one day before baking.

3 cups granulated sugar
2 cups milk
1 1/2 cups vegetable oil
3 eggs
1 1/4 cups chopped dried apricots
1/2 cup chopped peeled apples
1 tbsp vanilla
4 cups all-purpose flour
2 cups whole wheat flour
2 cups sour cream
1 1/2 tbsp baking powder
1 tbsp baking soda

In bowl, beat together sugar, milk, oil, eggs, apricots, apples and vanilla until well mixed.

In separate bowl, stir together all-purpose and whole wheat flours, sour cream, baking powder and baking soda. Stir into fruit mixture just until combined (do not overmix). Spoon into greased or paper-lined muffin cups, filling three-quarters full. Bake in 375°F oven for 30 to 35 minutes. Makes 36 muffins.

PUMPKIN CRANBERRY MUFFINS
Jakobstettel Guest House
Owner/Chef: Ella Brubacher

The unique combination of pumpkin and cranberry makes flavourful muffins.

4 eggs
2 cups granulated sugar
1 3/4 cups pumpkin (14 oz can)
1 1/2 cups vegetable oil
3 cups all-purpose flour
1 tbsp cinnamon
2 tsp baking powder
2 tsp baking soda
1 tsp salt
2 cups dried or frozen cranberries, cut in half

Beat eggs slightly. Add sugar, pumpkin and oil; beat well. Add flour, cinnamon, baking powder, baking soda and salt; mix until smooth. Stir in cranberries.

Spoon into greased muffin cups, filling two-thirds full. Bake in 375°F oven for 15 to 20 minutes. Makes 24 muffins.

St. Jacobs

SMOKED BACON CORN BREAD WITH ROOT CELLAR VEGETABLE SLATHER

The Pillar and Post Inn
Executive Chef: Virginia Marr

This superb bread, served with the vegetable slather, is a terrific accompaniment to a hearty winter stew or soup. Chef Marr serves the vegetable slather hot or cold. The chicken broth used to cook the vegetables can be saved to make soup.

Smoked Bacon Corn Bread

1 cup (approx) cornmeal
1/2 cup all-purpose flour
1 cup diced cooked smoked bacon
1/4 cup chopped fresh parsley
2 tsp baking powder
1 tsp salt
1/2 tsp baking soda
3/4 tsp cayenne pepper
1 1/4 cups buttermilk
2 large eggs
1/4 cup olive oil
1 cup freshly grated Parmesan cheese

Lightly grease loaf pan and sprinkle liberally with cornmeal to coat sides and bottom.

In bowl, combine 1 cup cornmeal, flour, bacon, parsley, baking powder, salt, baking soda and cayenne.

In small bowl, stir together buttermilk, eggs and oil. Add to flour mixture and stir just until blended. Stir in Parmesan cheese.

Pour batter into prepared loaf pan and bake in 350°F oven for 40 to 45 minutes or until tester inserted in centre comes out clean.

Root Cellar Vegetable Slather

1 small rutabaga, peeled and diced
2 parsnips, peeled and diced
2 carrots, peeled and sliced
1 Yukon Gold potato, peeled and diced
chicken broth
2 tbsp unsalted butter
2 tsp rosemary oil
salt and pepper

In saucepan over medium-high heat, combine rutabaga, parsnips, carrots and potatoes; pour in enough chicken broth to cover. Bring to boil. Cook, uncovered, until fork tender. Strain and mash with potato masher. When smooth, stir in butter, rosemary oil and salt and pepper to taste. Place in crock or ramekins and serve with cornbread. Makes about 3 to 4 cups.

Pillar & Post

ADELAIDE'S NOVA SCOTIA BROWN BREAD
Idlewyld Inn
Baker: Doug Huskilson
Village Harvest

The baker's great-grandmother made this bread for her turn-of-the-century family. Her granddaughter, Adelaide, often made it for her children's return from a day at the neighbourhood rink. Serve it with a winter stew or big pot of baked beans.

1 cup quick-cooking rolled oats (not instant)
2 1/2 to 3 cups warm water
1 pkg active dry yeast
2 cups whole wheat flour
2 cups all-purpose flour
1/3 cup blackstrap molasses (or 1/2 cup light molasses)
1 tbsp salt
1 tbsp brown sugar
1 tbsp canola or vegetable oil
butter

Soak rolled oats in 1/2 cup of the water for 30 minutes. Dissolve yeast according to package instructions. Gradually mix together oats, yeast, whole wheat and all-purpose flours, molasses, salt, sugar and oil, slowly adding 2 cups of the water and thoroughly mixing. If dough is stiff, add remaining 1/2 cup water. Knead intensely for 8 to 10 minutes. Dust lightly with flour. Transfer to bowl and cover with plastic wrap. Let stand in a warm place for about 1 hour or until doubled in size.

Punch down dough and form into 4 balls. Place 2 in 1 5- x 9-inch large loaf pan. In second loaf pan, place other 2 balls. Brush lightly with oil. Cover with large mixing bowl, being careful not to let it touch rising dough; let stand in warm place for about 15 minutes or until imprint remains in dough after touching lightly. Bake in 350°F oven for about 40 minutes.

Once baked, pull two loaves apart. Brush with butter and serve warm. Makes 4 loaves.

Chef's tip: Because bread is so dense, you may want to rotate the pans in oven every 15 minutes to ensure uniformity.

MUESLI BREAD
Idlewyld Inn
Baker: Doug Huskilson
Village Harvest

The Idlewyld Inn's freshly baked breads are supplied by a small local bakery called Village Harvest. This is one of those breads with something for everyone — cereals, fruits and nuts. It's a nutritious bread for people on the run.

1 cup muesli
2 1/2 to 3 cups water at room temperature
1 pkg active dry yeast
2 1/2 cups all-purpose flour
2 1/2 cups whole wheat flour
1 cup shelled sunflower seeds
1 tbsp brown sugar
1 tbsp canola or vegetable oil
1 tbsp salt
1 tsp cinnamon

Soak muesli in 1/2 cup of the water for 1 hour. Dissolve yeast according to package instructions. Gradually mix together muesli mixture, yeast, all-purpose and whole wheat flours, sunflower seeds, sugar, oil, salt and cinnamon, slowly adding 2 cups of the water and thoroughly mixing. If dough is stiff, add remaining 1/2 cup water. Knead aggressively for 5 minutes. Form into ball and dust lightly with flour. Transfer to bowl and cover with plastic wrap. Let rise in warm place for about 1 hour or until doubled in size.

Shape into 3 cylinders and place in large 5- x 9-inch loaf pans. Cover and let rise for another 30 minutes or until imprint remains in dough after touching lightly.

Bake in 375°F oven for about 40 minutes or until bottoms sound hollow when tapped. Remove from pans and let cool on racks. Makes 3 loaves.

PROFILES

In the course of researching this book, I visited many fine inns and restaurants. The 44 establishments that were selected for inclusion are profiled on the following pages.

When it comes to dining and accommodation, people have varied tastes. Some of the restaurants I have chosen are formal while others have a more casual, relaxed mood. The inns are all elegant in their own way and range in size from 4 to 138 guest rooms.

I hope you will enjoy visiting the establishments I have chosen. The accompanying information is up-to-date at the time of printing, but please remember that inn and restaurant ownership does change and chefs do move on to other places.

ANTHONY'S SEAFOOD BISTRO ●1

Anthony's Seafood Bistro has been London's premier seafood restaurant for over sixteen years. The combination of an open kitchen, innovative and consistently award-winning cooking, and an inviting atmosphere has made it a London highlight where the breads and desserts are as delicious as the seafood. The bistro's "trust me" dinner concept — a four-course surprise dinner — is a wonderful way to enjoy an evening at Anthony's. Chef/owner David Chapman and his wife, Karen, have surrounded themselves with warm and professional staff who treat new and old customers alike to a high level of service.

434 Richmond Street
London, ON
N6A 3C9
Telephone/fax: (519) 679-0960

Open year-round
Closed Sunday
Dinner: Monday through Saturday
Lunch: Monday through Friday
Restaurateurs: David and Karen Chapman

BAILEY'S RESTAURANT ●2

Located in the centre of Goderich, opposite the courthouse, Bailey's is housed in a 150-year-old building. Wrought iron fencing laced with ivy surrounds the restaurant's front outdoor patio while the interior features antiques and floor-length dusty rose tablecloths.

The wonderfully eclectic cuisine at Bailey's is changed daily. Owner/chef Ben Merritt creates such lunch specialties as steak and kidney pie, baked goat cheese in phyllo pastry on a bed of mixed lettuces, or saffron-scented seafood chowder. Dinner specialties could include fresh atlantic salmon with lobster cream sauce or succulent roast rack of lamb in a port wine jus.

120 The Courthouse Square
Goderich, ON
N7A 1M8
Telephone: (519) 524-5166

Open year-round
Closed Sunday
Lunch and Dinner: Tuesday through Saturday
Lunch Only: Monday
Restaurateur: Ben Merritt

BEILD HOUSE COUNTRY INN ●3

This grand home was built at the turn of the century for Dr. Joseph Arthur. Named Beild House, after the Gaelic word for shelter, the property has since been converted into a twelve-room country inn and restaurant.

Each of the guest rooms features its own unique decor with a gentle blending of antique furnishings and modern amenities. The living room is spacious and warmed by two fireplaces, and spa treatments can be enjoyed right on-site. The dining room is elegant and the breakfast menu features homemade preserves, seasonal fruit and a selection of hot dishes. An English-style afternoon sweet tea is served daily in the

Beild House Country Inn

library, and boxed lunches for the inn's outdoor adventures are also provided. The dinner menu includes Chef Bill's creative five-course dinners. Both breakfast and dinner are available to off-site diners with a reservation.

64 Third Street
Collingwood, ON
L9Y 1K5
Telephone: (705) 444-1522 or 1-888-322-3453
Fax: (705) 444-2394
E-mail: beildhouse@georgian.net
Web site: www.georgian.net/beildhouse

Open year-round
Innkeepers: Bill and Stephanie Barclay

BENMILLER INN

Housed in five strikingly-restored pioneer mills and mill owners' homes, the Benmiller Inn offers forty-seven guest rooms furnished with antiques and handmade quilts. Many rooms have balconies overlooking the Maitland river. The inn's indoor and outdoor amenities include a fitness centre with indoor pool, whirlpool and sauna, a games room with billiards and darts, and full spa services.

The Benmiller's Ivey Dining Room, open to inn guests and walk-in diners for breakfast, lunch, and dinner, is perched over the tumbling waters of Sharpe's Creek. Local Huron County products such as beef, trout, rabbit, maple syrup and berries are key ingredients in the menu. Chef Derek Griffiths's emphasis is on presenting a light naturally flavoured cuisine.

RR#4
Goderich, ON
N7A 3Y1
Telephone: (519) 524-2191 or 1-800-265-1711
Fax: (519) 524-5150
E-mail: benmillerinn@odyssey.on.ca

Open year-round
Innkeepers: Kathy Nichol and Randy Stoddart

Benmiller Inn

BHIMA'S WARUNG INTERNATIONAL 5

The restaurant name derives from "Bhima," a god in the famous Hindu epic "The Mahabarahta," who had a special talent for cooking and hosting large gatherings and whose name, coincidentally, is similar to that of Chef/owner Paul Boehmer. Paul was born locally, but spent many years travelling and apprenticing in the techniques of classical and modern cookery in Canada, the United States, Europe, and Asia. He acquired ancient recipes from an interesting variety of relatives from Afghanistan to Sri Lanka to Vietnam.

Located in a two-storey office building, this sixty-seat restaurant looks unassuming, but in fact conceals another world of sights, smells, and tastes. Beginning with classic South East Asian recipes, Bhima's makes them unique by marrying French techniques with Canadian ingredients, such as wild caribou and local rack of lamb. The seasonal specials include exotic tropical fish and the menu is complemented by a large selection of privately-stocked Asian beers, a good wine cellar, and exotic fruit drinks.

262 King Street North
Waterloo, ON
N2J 2Y9
Telephone: (519) 747-0722

Open year-round
Closed Monday
Dinner: Tuesday through Sunday
Hosts: Paul Boehmer and Nicole Helbig

BLACKSHOP RESTAURANT & LOUNGE 6

The Blackshop Restaurant got its name from its previous location, decorated to resemble a European blacksmith shop. Today, it is housed in an elegant stone building in historic downtown Galt. The main dining room seats sixty-five and is complimented by a fireplace lounge with a lovely cherry-wood bar. There is also a large private room for cocktail parties, weddings, seminars, or special functions.

The Blackshop features casual dining with European flair. Continental cuisine is its specialty, but the kitchen produces everything from calamari, to lamb, to burgers. The restaurant's atmosphere is comfortable and appealing and service is friendly and professional. An extensive wine list offers approximately 100 wines from around the world.

Blackshop Restaurant & Lounge

20 Hobson Street
Cambridge, ON
N1S 2M6
Telephone: (519) 621-4180
Fax: (519) 621-9128

Open year-round
Dinner: open daily
Lunch: Monday through Saturday
Restaurateurs: the Cerny Family

THE CHURCH RESTAURANT

The Church Restaurant is located near the Avon Theatre in downtown Stratford. It is housed in a historic building that dates back more than a century, when, in 1874, the congregation held its first service. Dwindling membership took its toll over the years and in 1975 the building was purchased and reopened as The Church Restaurant.

Diners enjoy the original architecture, stain glass windows, organ pipes, and a gracious

DA CARUSO RISTORANTE

Located in a Tudor-style town house, circa 1850, da Caruso Ristorante opened its doors in the fall of 1995. Proprietor Diana Caruso, from Friuli, Italy, executes both pride and expertise when choosing the finest imported goods and fresh local produce for her restaurant.

Colourful frescoed interiors painted by Diana's daughter Gabriella form the perfect backdrop for a menu boasting fresh grilled seafood, antipasto, and authentic regional pasta. da Caruso has received favourable reviews from *Toronto Life* and a number of local publications for both its culinary fare and friendly, knowledgeable staff. Diners enjoy the restaurant's licensed patio, in warmer months, and intimate candlelight tables inside the town house throughout the year.

26 Church Street
St. Catharines, ON
L2R 3B6
Telephone: (905) 641-0279

Open year-round
Closed Sunday and Monday
Lunch and Dinner: Tuesday through Saturday
Licensed patio: from May 24
Restaurateur: Diana Caruso

atmosphere that equals the fine food and thoughtful service. The menu, innovatively French, also reflects executive chef and co-owner Sheldon Russell's interest in global foods.

Upstairs, the Belfry Restaurant and Bar offers a more cosy and less formal dining area, yet with the same level of service and interesting menu selections. All dishes are prepared with the freshest ingredients, using organic foods and local produce. An extensive wine list chosen by co-owner and general manager Mark Craft complements the menu.

70 Brunswick Street
Stratford, Ontario
N5A 6V6
Telephone: (519) 273-3424
Fax: (519) 272-0061
E-mail: churchrest@orc.ca

Open May 6 to November 5
Closed Monday
Lunch: Wednesday, Saturday and Sunday
Dinner: Tuesday through Sunday
General Manager: Mark Craft

DEVLINS COUNTRY BISTRO

704 Mount Pleasant Road
Mount Pleasant, ON
N0E 1K0
Telephone: (519) 484-2258
Fax: (519) 484-2037

Open year-round
Closed Sunday
Dinner: Monday through Saturday
Lunch: Friday
Restaurateur: Chris Devlin

ELM HURST INN

Beginning in 1884, five generations of Devlin's operated Mount Pleasant's General Store and Post Office. When it closed in 1990, Chris Devlin transformed the old store into a restaurant. Devlin's is now a pretty, white-framed building situated in Mount Pleasant, a small Ontario town in the countryside south of Brantford. The interior is relaxed yet elegant and features original art by local artists.

Devlin's delicious contemporary Italian cuisine uses today's modern flavours and products, and makes use of seasonal local products when available. Diners will enjoy specialties such as grilled sea scallops with capellini and Asian stir-fry, oven roasted veal tenderloin with a Merlot wine sauce and garlic spinach, or a mixed grill created nightly. Bread is baked in the kitchen every morning.

This Victorian Gothic home was built in 1872 as a residence for James Harris, a prominent fruit and dairy merchant. Today, the inn's forty-nine individually decorated rooms and suites have a subtle blend of country charm and modern amenities. Some of the activities available to visitors include swimming, ice skating, badminton, and billiards. Additional facilities include a fitness centre, hiking trails, and spa.

The Elm Hurst's dining room is very gracious and offers a monthly schedule of theme dinners, such as Greek or Asian nights and Sunday evening roast beef dinners. The inn's well-known Sunday brunch includes a seafood and salad table, freshly carved roasts, and dozens of choices of sweets. The buffet is accompanied by live music, usually violin or classical guitar. Off-site guests are welcome.

Elm Hurst Inn

Highways 401 and 19
Ingersoll, ON
N5C 3K1
Telephone: (519) 485-5321 or 1-800-561-5321
Fax: (519) 485-6579

Open year-round
Lunch and Dinner: daily
Sunday brunch
Innkeeper: Pat Davies

ELORA MILL INN

The Elora Mill, a 150-year-old grist mill turned country inn, has a dramatic setting, towering above the thundering falls of the Grand River. There are thirty-two uniquely designed rooms and suites divided among four historic buildings in the heart of Ontario's festival country.

The Mill's fireside dining room overlooks the roaring falls. The menu is based around a cornucopia of local foods — trout, apples, cheeses, maple syrup, lamb, and organically-grown produce — and is complemented by an excellent wine list praised for its wide range of Ontario wines. The Innkeeper's Breakfast, which is included with an overnight stay, features granola and preserves.

77 Mill Street West,
Elora, ON
N0B 1S0
Telephone: (519) 846-5356
Fax: (519) 846-9180

Open year-round
Lunch and Dinner: daily
Innkeeper: Jennifer Smith

ENVER'S

Enver's is housed in an old stone building situated in the hamlet of Morriston, a short drive from Guelph or Hamilton. An intimate fifty-seat restaurant, Enver's has achieved the feeling of Provence.

The fare is international in flavour, using Far East and New World spicing. Enver's is noted for its extensive wine list, which features a wide variety of offerings from Niagara and California.

Highway 6
Morriston, ON
N0B 2C0
Telephone: (519) 821-2852
Fax: (519) 821-5657

Open year-round
Closed Monday
Lunch and Dinner: Tuesday to Friday
Dinner only: Saturday
Brunch: Sunday
Restaurateur: Enver Bismallah

THE EPICUREAN 13

The Epicurean is located on the main street of historic Niagara-on-the-Lake. Casual surroundings provide a friendly backdrop for the homemade fare. An outdoor patio in the middle of an English garden at the back of the restaurant offers a bistro menu for lunch or dinner or the perfect spot to sip a cool drink in the afternoon.

The decor is very Provençal, but the menu features a variety of Mediterranean influences. Some of owner/chef Ruth Aspinall's specialties include wild mushroom lasagne with red pepper sauce, a variety of focaccia made on the premises with a choice of fillings such as grilled rosemary chicken, olive tapenade, tomatoes with lemon dressing, or roman grilled portobello mushrooms, sun-dried tomatoes, carmelized onions, and asiago cheese. Thursday, Friday, and Saturday evenings feature live jazz performances.

84 Queen Street
Niagara-on-the-Lake, ON
L0S 1J0
Telephone: (905) 468-3408

Open mid March to December 31
Lunch and Dinner: daily
Takeout and picnic baskets available
Restaurateurs: Scott and Ruth Aspinall

GLENERIN INN 14

Glenerin Inn was originally built in 1927 for William Watson Evans, a wealthy Toronto businessman, as a summer retreat for his family. Rescued from demolition in 1984, the Glenerin now stands proudly as one of Mississauga's most elegant and architecturally significant historic sites.

A blend of old world charm and modern amenities, Glenerin's houses a lobby that is grand, yet warm and cozy. There are thirty-nine guest rooms and suites, each uniquely furnished with period antiques and reproductions. Fireplaces and private whirlpool baths are found in some suites, and the inn offers conference rooms in a variety of sizes.

Breakfast, lunch, and dinner are served in the inn's restaurant, Thatcher's, for inn guests and walk-in diners. In the warmer months, guests

enjoy dining on the covered patio garden overlooking the Sawmill Valley Conservation Area and its beautiful wooded walking trails.

1695 The Collegeway
Mississauga, ON
L5L 3S7
Telephone/fax: (905) 828-6103
Reservations: 1-800-267-0525
Open year-round
Innkeeper: Geoff Slater

GROSVENOR'S OF SOUTHAMPTON

Grosvenor's restaurant is located in the town of Southampton, on the eastern shore of Lake Huron. Southampton is the oldest port on the Bruce County coast. Situated in the old Canadian National Railway station, built in 1906, the restaurant has a unique and charming character.

Chef Paul Johnston features innovative regional Canadian cuisine. Local wild game, fish, meats, housemade pastas, gourmet breads, and pastries are all prepared for dinner guests within the walls of his kitchen. After working several years in Michelin-rated restaurants throughout Europe, Johnston has returned home to Southampton. He describes Bruce County as Ontario's best kept secret and insists that "the local products available here are better than any other place I have ever worked or lived."

P.O. Box 1147
124 Grosvenor Street South
Southampton, ON
N0H 2L0
Telephone/fax: (519) 797-1226

Dinner (daily): May through September, December

Dinner (Thursday through Sunday): October, November, January through April
Restaurateurs: Paul and Jacqueline Johnston

HILLEBRAND'S VINEYARD CAFÉ

Hillebrand Estates Winery is located at the centre of Niagara's wine country, but visitors are free to do much more than just taste wines. A winery tour including a tutored tasting of Hillebrand's latest VQA wines is one way to enjoy the property. Guests can also browse the rare vintages in the Wine Boutique, take a vineyard bicycle tour or attend one of the winery's many special events.

Hillebrand's Vineyard Café is built into the very heart of the winery, overlooking the barrel cellar and the vineyards. Its wall of windows creates a very open and airy feeling and offers a spectacular view of the Niagara Escarpment. Chef Antonio de Luca's approach to wine country cuisine utilizes fresh seasonal ingredients from the area. His philosophy is to accent the true flavours of foods and to marry suitable combinations.

Hwy 55, off the Q.E.W.
Niagara-on-the-Lake, ON
L0S 1J0
Telephone: (905) 468-2444 or 1 (800) 582-8412
Fax: (905) 468-4789
Web site: www.hillebrand.com

Open year-round
Winemaker: J-L Groux
Chef: Antonio de Luca

Hillebrand's Vineyard Café

IDLEWYLD INN 17

Idlewyld Inn was built in 1878 as a residence for Charles S. Hyman, a wealthy London businessman, sportsman, and politician. Today, this bed-and-breakfast is situated in a residential London neighbourhood, minutes from downtown shops, theatres, and restaurants. The decor is elegant and charming. Ornate wood mouldings, intricately carved fireplaces, and a massive central staircase have all been meticulously restored. Each of the twenty-seven guest rooms boasts its own unique decor — a subtle blending of antique furnishings and modern amenities — and some contain whirlpools and fireplaces. The inn's gracious living room invites guests to relax by the fireplace and be swept away by the surroundings. Each morning a light breakfast is served in the lovely breakfast room or on the garden patio.

Idlewyld Inn has private facilities to accommodate up to sixty people for catered business meetings, social functions, or weddings.

36 Grand Avenue
London, ON
N6C 1K8
Telephone/fax: (519) 433-2891

Open year-round
Innkeeper: Dawn Lashbrook

JAKOBSTETTEL GUEST HOUSE 18

Located in the town of St. Jacobs, Jakobstettel is a close walk to shops, restaurants, and cultural attractions. Refurbished in 1982, this Victorian-style bed-and-breakfast has twelve gracious guest rooms with private baths, situated on five treed acres that offer an outdoor pool, tennis court, and bikes for guest use.

The lounge and library are restful areas, ideal for reading, and guests are lured to the kitchen, where there's always fresh baking offered. Jakobstettel serves breakfast only, which includes muffins, locally-made Jersey Cheddar, fresh fruit, homemade granola and preserves, coffee, tea, and juice. Within walking distance are excellent dining choices and fabulous shopping for handmade crafts, gifts, and gourmet treats.

16 Isabella Street
St. Jacobs, ON
N0B 2N0
Telephone: (519) 664-2208
Fax: (519) 664-1326

Open year-round
Lunch and Dinner: available to groups in the meeting room, by reservation
Innkeeper: Ella Brubacher

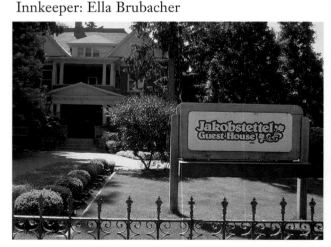

JANET LYNN'S BISTRO

Janet and Kevin are the husband and wife team of Janet Lynn's Bistro in uptown Waterloo. Janet is the chef and Kevin is the restaurant manager and sommelier.

The restaurant is casually elegant and beautifully designed with four English garden murals painted by renowned local artist, Peter Etril Snyder.

The cuisine is fresh market with French and Italian influences. The delicious and wonderfully presented menu selections are changed seasonally and may include corn-fed chicken stuffed with organic spinach, mascarpone cheese with fettuccine and morels, and grilled lamb tenderloin with feta cheese, onion confit, kalamata olives, and warm marinated beets. The wine list hosts a selection of over 100 vintage wines and reserve (rare) wines on request.

92 King Street South
Waterloo, ON
N2J 1P5
Telephone: (519) 725-3440
Fax: (519) 725-5580

Open year-round
Closed Sunday
Lunch and Dinner: Monday through Friday
Dinner Only: Saturday
Restaurateur: Janet Leslie and Kevin Wong

KETTLE CREEK INN

Kettle Creek Inn is nestled in the heart of Port Stanley's small fishing village on Lake Erie's north shore. The inn, built in 1849, consists of five luxury suites with whirlpools, baths, gas fireplaces, living rooms, and private balconies, as well as ten unique guest rooms with private baths. Guests can relax by the fire in the cosy parlour, have a drink in the pub, or dine in the relaxed European bistro atmosphere of one of three dining rooms. During fair weather, gazebo and patio tables are also available. Off-site guests are welcome for lunch and dinner.

Chef Frank Hubert creates such fresh market dinner specialties as locally-raised rhea (similar to an ostrich, though slightly smaller), fresh perch, pickerel, trout, and Brome Lake duck.

The community offers such activities as sailing and fishing charters, two sandy beaches, summer theatre, tours of the historic Port Stanley Terminal Railway, golf courses, hiking, and bird-watching.

216 Joseph Street
Port Stanley, ON
N5L 1C4
Telephone: (519) 782-3388
Fax: (519) 782-4747
E-mail: kci@webgate.net

Open year-round
Lunch and Dinner: seven days a week
Innkeepers: Jean Strickland and Gary Vedova

KEYSTONE ALLEY CAFÉ 21

"The Keystone," as the locals fondly refer to it, is located near Stratford's Avon Theatre and unique shops.

A café by day; a dining experience by night is an apt description for this popular restaurant. The luncheon menu offers homemade soups, salads, pastas, and sandwiches. The dinner menu, with a French influence, pays close attention to fresh ingredients and presentation. The desserts are delectable. With an open kitchen concept, the Keystone has an atmosphere that is relaxed and its service is attentive. Under the watchful eye of executive chef and co-owner Sheldon Russell, the fifteen-year-old restaurant has become a favourite with locals and visitors alike.

34 Brunswick Street
Stratford, ON
N5A 3L8
Telephone: (519) 271-5645

Open year-round
Closed Sunday
Lunch: Monday through Saturday
Dinner: Tuesday through Saturday
Restaurateurs: Mark Craft and Sheldon Russel

THE KIELY INN & TAPESTRIES RESTAURANT

The Kiely Inn was built in 1832 as a family home by Charles Richardson. It is a superb example of post and beam construction and there are many features of historical and architectural interest, which are protected by a historic designation. This magnificent late-Georgian house has eleven guest rooms decorated in the style of the period with antiques and delicately coloured wallpaper. Half of the rooms have wood-burning fireplaces. The Kiely Inn is situated on Niagara-on-the-Lake's main street on one acre of lawns and gardens, overlooking a golf course and Lake Ontario. It is within walking distance to the Shaw Theatre and shops.

Tapestries Restaurant is housed in two rooms, both of which have a formal, elegant ambiance with large wood-burning fireplaces and fine mirrors gracing their mantels. The dining rooms are almost unchanged from their original state, and the central gaseliers, suspended staircase, and curved door are all of interest. The cuisine is Continental with a Mediterranean flair, using fresh Niagara ingredients.

209 Queen Street
Niagara-on-the-Lake, ON
L0S 1J0
Telephone: (905) 468-4588
Fax: (905) 468-2194

Open year-round
Innkeepers: Ray and Heather Pettit

LA CACHETTE

La Cachette is situated next to the Grand River in a new stone-faced building designed to match the rest of the town's old masonry. In the warm season, guests can enjoy dining on the patio overlooking the river. The casual, intimate, deep red-toned dining room has a fireplace and large windows also facing the Grand River.

Co-owner/chef Alain Levesque's seasonal lunch and dinner menus offer deliciously light Provençal cuisine, with vegetarian and seafood dishes as well as chicken, pork, and beef. Grilled vegetables to match the season are always a delight. An after-dinner cigar can be enjoyed in La Cachette's cosy lounge.

13 Mill Street East
Elora, ON
N0B 1S0
Telephone: (519) 846-8346

Seasonal:
Victoria Day to Labour Day
Lunch and Dinner: daily
Labour Day to Thanksgiving
Closed Monday
Lunch and Dinner: Tuesday through Sunday
Thanksgiving to Victoria Day
Closed Monday and Tuesday

Lunch and Dinner: Wednesday through Sunday
Restaurateurs: Patricia Keyes and Alain Levesque

LAKEWINDS COUNTRY MANOR

Lakewinds was built in 1881 as a summer home for Mr. Gustav Fleischmann of the famous Fleischmann's yeast company in Buffalo, New York. Over 100 years later, Jane and Steve Locke restored and opened this Niagara-on-the-Lake mansion as a bed-and-breakfast. Lakewinds is situated on a quiet acre of extensive flower gardens and mature trees. There is a heated outdoor pool, a games room, and a solarium. Guests enjoy a beautiful view of the golf course beside Lake Ontario. A short stroll away is the centre of old Niagara-on-the-Lake, where Lakewind's patrons will find theatres, shops, and restaurants.

Common areas of the manor are elegantly appointed with an eclectic mix of antiques and other period furniture. All guest rooms are uniquely decorated and have ensuite bathrooms.

Sumptuous breakfasts, using fresh herbs and produce from the garden, are served in the manor's grand dining room, or you may have a continental breakfast delivered to your room.
P.O. Box 1483
328 Queen Street
Niagara-on-the-Lake, ON
L0S 1J0
Telephone: (905) 468-1888
Fax: (905) 468-1061
Web site: www.lakewinds.niagara.com

Open year-round
Innkeepers: Jane and Stephen Locke

Lakewinds, Niagara-on-the-Lake

LANGDON HALL

Langdon Hall was built in 1898 by Eugene Langdon Wilks, the great grandson of American financier John Jacob Astor. This impressive American Federal Revival house is located near Cambridge and situated among 200 acres of gardens and woodlands. Langdon Hall now consists of forty elegant guest rooms and three suites, each with its own charm. Amenities include walking trails, lawn croquet, tennis courts, a swimming pool, sauna, whirlpool, exercise room, and spa services.

The dining room offers regional dishes and classical cuisine, served in an atmosphere of warmth and elegance overlooking the lily pond and gardens. The menu is rich in Langdon Hall's own products, such as honey, apples, vegetables, and herbs, grown on the estate. Lunch and dinner are also available in the relaxed atmosphere of the lovely Wilks Bar.

R.R. 33
Cambridge, ON
N3H 4R8
Telephone: (519) 740-2100 or 1-800-268-1898
Fax: (519) 740-8161

Open year-round
Innkeepers: Bill Bennett and Mary Beaton

THE LITTLE INN OF BAYFIELD

The Little Inn of Bayfield has been welcoming guests to its two-storey gingerbread embellished porch since 1832. Located on Bayfield's heritage main street, the inn is just a few minutes away from the golden sand beaches of Lake Huron, where boating and water sports can be enjoyed in season. In fall and winter, The Little Inn is a popular destination for hikers, cross-country skiers, and snowshoers. The thirty rooms are individually decorated with unique beds and antique furnishings, many with ensuite whirlpools and fireplaces. Guests can relax by the fire in the gracious lounge or enjoy a drink in the cosy bar.

The inn's brick and pine heritage dining room with large picture windows overlooking the gardens gives one the feeling of rural Ontario. Imaginative menus featuring continental cuisine are constantly changing and always include local country grown-and-raised produce from Huron County. Some specialties include roast three-peppercorn-crusted rack of lamb, oven-roasted Lake Huron whitefish, or seared Lake Huron pickerel fillet with shallot, garlic, and Merlot sauce. Off-site guests are welcome for lunch and dinner. The Little Inn has won two consecutive Awards of Excellence from the *Wine Spectator* for the over 230 types of wines in its cellar.

Main Street
Bayfield, ON
N0M 1G0
Telephone: (519) 565-2611 or 1-800-565-1832
Fax: (519) 565-5474

The Little Inn of Bayfield

Open year-round
Innkeepers: Patrick and Gayle Waters

THE OLD PRUNE RESTAURANT

The Old Prune is set in a quiet Edwardian house, with tables clustered in three cozy rooms complimented by original art and large windows. A patio overlooks a secluded garden where one can take in the aromas of bread baking in the ovens and salmon smoking in the hothouse.

Using the finest and freshest ingredients raised by a dedicated community of organic farmers in the region, Chef Bryan Steele creates a cuisine of natural simplicity and abundant flavour. The service is professional. The wine list carries carefully selected vintages from right across the map and price range. Canadian wines are marketed with as much confidence as any others.

151 Albert Street
Stratford, ON
N5A 3K5
Telephone: (519) 271-5052
Fax: (519) 271-4157
E-mail: oldprune@cyg.net

Open May to October
Closed Monday
Dinner: Tuesday through Sunday
Lunch: Wednesday through Sunday
Restaurateurs: Marion Isherwood and Eleanor Kane

THE OTHER BROTHER'S RESTAURANT

The Other Brother's Restaurant has been located in Guelph's old Raymond Sewing Machine factory since October, 1995. Inside, the dining room is elegant and inviting, decorated in dusty rose tones with leather sofas around the fireplace. The tables are situated to ensure privacy, and quiet areas and separate rooms are available for small private parties or business discussions.

The menu focuses on classically prepared dishes with some international flavours, and the decadent desserts all made in-house. The menu features such specialties as sesame smoked fillet of salmon, twice-cooked crispy skinned duck, and cumin-crusted tuna. A three-course fondue dinner is served by reservation only.

The Other Brother's was honoured in 1997 as the "Best Fine Food Restaurant in North America" by Elan International Brands and was rated with two out of three stars — among the top sixty restaurants in the country — in Anne Hardy's *Where to Eat in Canada*.

37 Yarmouth Street
Guelph, ON
N1H 4G2
Telephone/fax: (519) 822-4465

Open year-round
Lunch: Tuesday through Friday
Dinner: Monday through Saturday
Restaurateurs: Sara Watson and Karim Ladhani

PARADISO

Paradiso is located in downtown Old Oakville. The interior is whimsical with ochre washes over artfully distressed surfaces, spotted stars, moons, and sculptural oddities.

While the surroundings represent a labour of love, the menu itself reflects a love of food.

Paradiso, which describes its cuisine as "Mediterranean confluence," uses fresh, high-quality food prepared in ways that highlight the natural flavours. Julia Hanna, the owner and proprietor, and Michael Killip, the chef, share a vision of good food served without pretension. The atmosphere and open kitchen create a feeling of live entertainment nightly at the chef's tables. There is an extensive wine list.

125 Lakeshore Road East
Oakville, ON
L6L 1H3
Telephone: (905) 338-1594
Fax: (905) 338-8245

Open year-round
Lunch and Dinner: daily
Restaurateur: Julia Hanna

THE PILLAR AND POST INN

The Pillar and Post Inn, Spa and Conference Centre is located in a quiet residential area, and is only a ten-minute walk from Niagara-on-the-Lake's main street. Originally built in the late 1800s as a canning factory in the midst of Niagara's fruit belt, it has since been transformed into a luxurious inn, with 123 individually decorated guest rooms, many with fireplaces, four-poster king-sized beds, and whirlpool tubs. Services and amenities include a business centre, thirteen conference/banquet rooms, a floral shop, a European spa and health club fitness centre, indoor and outdoor swimming pools, and an outdoor whirlpool. Relax in front of a fire in the warm, gracious front lobby or enjoy a drink in The Vintages Wine Bar and Lounge.

Cosy fireside dining set in the casually elegant Carriages and Cannery Dining Rooms offers superb fresh market cuisine, featuring Niagara's finest produce. Full country breakfasts and buffets are also featured in both dining rooms. Off-site guests are welcome for breakfast, lunch, and dinner.

King Street at John Street
P.O. Box 1011
Niagara-on-the-Lake, ON
L0S 1J0
Telephone: (905) 468-2123 or 1-800-361-6788
Fax: (905) 468-3551

Open year-round
Owner/operator: Si Wai Lai

THE PRINCE OF WALES HOTEL

Established in 1864, the Prince of Wales Hotel is one of Niagara-on-the-Lake's most historic

landmarks. Situated on the town's main street, the Prince of Wales offers 101 elegant rooms, all retaining the charm of its Victorian origins. Standard and deluxe rooms are available, as well as a choice of newly redesigned one-bedroom suites.

Services and amenities include six conference/banquet rooms, a weight room, a sauna, a whirlpool, and an indoor pool.

The hotel's casually gracious Royals Dining Room overlooks beautiful Simcoe Park. Chef Ralf Bretzigheimer prepares exquisite classic fresh market cuisine with French influence. The wine cellar is stocked with vintage Niagara wines as well as an extensive selection of imports. Off-site guests are welcome for breakfast, lunch, and dinner.

6 Picton Street
Niagara-on-the-Lake, ON
L0S 1J0
Telephone: (905) 468-3246 or 1-800-263-2452
Fax: (905) 468-5521

Open year-round
Owner/operator: Si Wai Lai

QUEEN'S LANDING INN & CONFERENCE RESORT

Queen's Landing Inn & Conference Resort is a stately Georgian-style mansion, overlooking the scenic Niagara River and Lake Ontario, and minutes from Niagara-on-the-Lake's main street and Shaw Festival Theatre. Many of the 138 elegant rooms, each individually decorated, feature cosy fireplaces and whirlpool baths. Amenities include a fully-equipped exercise room, indoor pool, whirlpool, and sauna facilities. A Business Services Centre is also available, along with seventeen conference/banquet rooms.

Also overlooking the Niagara River, the inn's Tiara Restaurant is casually elegant with white columns and reproductions of seventeenth-century paintings. Tiara's team of award-winning chefs share a passion and appreciation for the creation of exquisitely prepared and presented eclectic cuisine. Some specialties are foie gras with Niagara peach preserve and toasted sour dough bread, Speck farm quail with soya and

Queen's Landing Inn

star anise, and oven-roasted Niagara peaches with vanilla bean and lime butter. Off-site guests are welcome for breakfast, lunch, and dinner.

155 Byron Street
P.O. Box 1180
Niagara-on-the-Lake, ON
L0S 1J0
Telephone: (905) 468-2195 or 1-800-361-6645
Fax: (905) 468-2227

Open year-round
Owner/operator: Si Wai Lai

RINDERLIN'S DINING ROOMS

Rinderlin's in Welland is housed in an historically designated building known as The Fortner House. This Queen Anne Revival-style building dates back to 1806, and was fully renovated to its original splendour in the early 1980s. The main floor houses six dining rooms and provides a total capacity of eighty-five seats. Three of the rooms showcase working fireplaces. The Rose Terrace, a sunny room favoured by luncheon guests, was fashioned from the original wrap-around veranda.

Rinderlin's features *à la minute* preparation of its European-inspired entrées, and includes techniques such as in-house hot smoking.

Everything is "made from scratch," including bases for soups or sauces, ice cream, and croissants. The menu features an extensive variety of vegetables, beef, poultry, pork, venison, game, and seafood.

24 Burgar Street
Welland, ON
L3B 2S7
Telephone: (905) 735-4411

Open year-round
Closed Sunday and Monday
Lunch: Tuesday through Friday
Dinner: Tuesday through Saturday
Restaurateur: Jan Newman

ROGUES

Rogues is tucked away in Mississauga's exclusive Sherwood Forrest Village shopping plaza. The interior reminds one of a European villa, with rosy brick, imported tiles, and a garden of greenery that separates the large restaurant into casual cozy niches dressed in white linen.

Restaurateur Tony Pereira — formerly of the Windsor Arms and the Millcroft Inn — will most likely be on hand to personally greet his patrons. Chefs Bevan Terry and Pascal Gendron love the open kitchen's proximity to guests every bit as much as the diners do. The menu offers

delicious and beautifully prepared northern Italian and continental specialties, such as veal scalloppini with lemon basil white wine sauce, capellini with roast garlic oil, pesto, sun-dried tomatoes and grilled chicken breast, and poached salmon in a smooth Chardonnay lemon lime butter sauce.

1900 Dundas Street West
Sherwood Forrest Shopping Village
Mississauga, ON
L5K 1P9
Telephone: (905) 822-2670
Fax: (905) 822-2677

Open year-round
Closed Sunday
Lunch: Monday through Friday
Dinner: Monday through Saturday
Restaurateur: Tony Pereira

RUNDLES 35

Rundles reflects the genuine passion for food and the arts of its soft-spoken owner, James Morris. It is located in a superbly decorated, summer-cool house, set by Stratford's pretty Avon River adrift with swans. The dining room is full of comforts with soft white cushions and numerous bouquets of beautiful flowers.

Rundles chef, Neil Baxter, has earned the attention of *Gourmet* and other important culinary magazines, with special tributes paid to his grilled vegetable terrine, crispy-skin *confit* of duck, beautiful grilled and cold-poached salmon, and seared shellfish coins. An international

selection of carefully chosen wines compliment the fine lunch and dinner menus.

9 Cobourg Street
Stratford, ON
N5A 3E4
Telephone: (519) 271-6442
Fax: (519) 271-3279

Open: May 24 to November 2
Closed Monday
Lunch: Wednesday, Saturday and Sunday
Dinner: Tuesday through Sunday
Restaurateur: James Morris

THE SCHOOLHOUSE COUNTRY INN 36 RESTAURANT

The Schoolhouse Country Inn Restaurant is situated in Belwood among two acres of gardens and woodlands. Finished in 1843, this the largest fieldstone schoolhouse built in Ontario. A circular gazebo adjoins a large wooden porch with comfortable chairs and views of the Grand River and Belwood Lake.

The ambiance is wonderfully romantic with lots of lace and a wood-burning fireplace. In fact, the Schoolhouse has been chosen "the area's most romantic restaurant" by *The Kitchener/*

Waterloo Record. The attractively presented regional cuisine includes entrées of venison, wild boar, tuna, rack of lamb, and beef tenderloin. Fine wines and a selection of over fifty single malt scotches are also found at this country restaurant.

Wellington Road 26
Belwood, ON
N0B 1J0
Telephone: (519) 843-3576
Web site: www. schoolhouseinn.com

Closed January
Open February through May
Lunch and dinner: Friday through Sunday
Open May through December
Lunch: Friday through Sunday
Dinner: Wednesday through Monday
Restaurateur: Peter Egger

STONE MAIDEN INN 37

The Stone Maiden Inn, built in 1872, is named for the carved stone figureheads which adorn the front hallway. This special bed-and-breakfast, located two blocks from downtown Stratford, has a fresh country atmosphere yet preserves its early Victorian elegance. Its fourteen comfortable guest rooms are decorated in soft colours with cosy quilts, pillows, and antiques. Fireplaces, whirlpool baths, and refrigerators are found in some rooms.

In the morning, guests can enjoy early coffee in their room, and a bountiful breakfast in the dining room. In the afternoon, patrons can relax in the comfortable lounge or outside on the veranda, where complimentary beverages and other treats are offered.

123 Church Street
Stratford, ON
N5A 2R3
Telephone: (519) 271-7129
Fax: (519) 271-4615

Open April through December
Innkeepers: Barb and Len Woodward

TRATTORIA IL TIMONE 38

Trattoria Il Timone is located in the heart of downtown old Oakville. The informal decor is Italian-inspired, with white stucco walls and dark wood. Quaint Mediterranean scenes are hand painted in semi-circular imitation windows, giving one the impression of a courtyard. On another wall, lovely bevelled windows open up onto the street in the warmer months. A black ceiling highlighted with hundreds of tiny white bulbs gives the feeling of dining under the stars.

The menu is dominated by northern Italian influences. Along with the regular menu, lunch and dinner daily specials are featured. These delicious specialties may include a variety of grilled fish such as Arctic char, salmon, grouper,

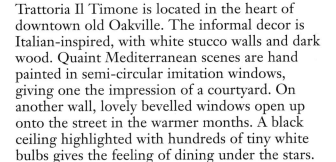

halibut, and tuna. Lamb loin in puff pastry with two sauces or homemade gnocchi with a rose tomato sauce surrounded by grilled sea scallops are two examples from Trattoria's list of entrées. A well-selected wine list including a great variety of vintage wines compliments the food. The service is friendly and attentive.

263 Lakeshore Road East
Oakville, ON
L6J 1H9
Telephone: (905) 842-2906
Open year-round
Closed Sunday
Lunch and Dinner: Monday through Saturday
Restaurateur: Allan Mickevicius

VINELAND ESTATES WINERY RESTAURANT

Vineland Estates Winery is set on a seventy-five-acre vineyard in Vineland, Ontario. Tastings are offered all year, seven days a week, and wine, wine accessories, and other gift items may be purchased from the Wineshop. From June 1 to October 31, you can take a tour of the winery, followed by a tasting.

The Vineland Estate restaurant is relaxed and elegant. It is fully enclosed by large glass windows, allowing guests a panoramic view of the vineyards and Lake Ontario. In the summer months, one can enjoy dining on the outdoor deck that's been built around a large, old tree. Chef Mark Picone's culinary talents ensure the finest in regional fresh market cuisine. Their quarterly menu changes reflect the harvesting of local fruits and vegetables.

3620 Moyer Road
Vineland, ON
L0R 2C0
Telephone: (905) 562-7088
Fax: (905) 562-3071
Web site: www.vineland.com

Open year-round
Lunch and Dinner: daily
Winemakers: Allan and Brian Schmidt
Chef: Mark Picone

VINTNER'S INN & ON THE TWENTY 40

Vintner's Inn is located in the town of Jordan on the second and third storeys of a renovated sugar warehouse that dates back to Niagara's earliest years as a wine growing region. The decor is luxurious with stone hearths and counters, classic columns, and refined colour schemes. There are sixteen elegant suites, half of them two-storey. The bi-level suites feature a living room, fireplace, and powder room on the lower level, and a bedroom and full bath with whirlpool on the upper level.

All guests are welcome to a winery tour and tasting at Cave Spring Cellars, located across the street from the inn. The quaint little village has a number of shops with unique products, including three antique stores. Cave Spring Cellars has a store offering fine wines and accessories.

Across the road from the inn is the inn's restaurant, On The Twenty. The restaurant has the feel of old Europe with warmth and elegance. It has beautiful stone and iron work and large displays of fresh herbs. Chef Michael Olsen is committed to using fresh, locally grown ingredients to develop a unique Niagara style of cooking that is superb.

3845 Main Street
Jordan, ON
L0R 1S0
Telephone: (905) 562-5336 or 1-800-701-8074
Fax: (905) 562-3232
E-mail: vintners@niagara.net

Open year-round
On the Twenty — Seasonal: January
Closed Monday through Wednesday
Lunch and Dinner: Thursday through Sunday,
February to April
Closed Monday
Lunch and Dinner: Tuesday through Sunday,
May to December
Lunch and Dinner: daily
Innkeeper: Helen Young

WELLINGTON COURT RESTAURANT

Located in the heart of Niagara's wine region,
Wellington Court is Edwardian in style on the
outside. Inside, the intimate jazz-filled dining
room offers a quaint setting in which to enjoy
the superb creations of one of Niagara's premier
chefs, Eric Peacock. Eric uses only the freshest
local ingredients to present a meal as pleasing to
the eye as it is to the palate.

   Established in 1985 by Claudia Peacock,
Wellington Court maintains a strong reputation

for excellent fine dining and service in a relaxed
atmosphere. It has enjoyed eight years of
recognition in Anne Hardy's
Where to Eat in Canada.

11 Wellington Street
St. Catharines, ON
L2R 5P5
Telephone/fax: (905) 682-5518

Open year-round
Lunch and Dinner: Monday
through Saturday
Restaurateur: Claudia
Peacock

THE WESTOVER INN

The Westover Inn began as a limestone
Victorian mansion, built in 1867 by William and
Joseph Hutton as their family home. One
hundred and twenty-seven years later, the inn
offers twenty-two charming guest rooms set on
nineteen acres of landscaped grounds. It is
located just twelve miles from Stratford, in the
town of St. Marys. Over the last ten years, The
Westover Inn has evolved into a destination for
Stratford Festival actors, such as Christopher
Plummer.

The Westover Inn

The Westover features two unique dining rooms and an outdoor patio serving exceptional regional cuisine. Chef Michael Hoy has shaped the inn's superb menu around locally grown ingredients. For the second year in a row, they have achieved a four-diamond CAA/AAA rating, and in 1997 they were awarded two stars out of three in Anne Hardy's *Where to Eat in Canada*.

300 Thomas Street
St. Marys, ON
N4X 1B1
Telephone: (519) 284-2977 or 1-800-cottage
Fax: (519)284-4043

Open year-round
Innkeepers: Julie Docker and Stephen McCotter

THE WILDFLOWER RESTAURANT 43

The Wildflower is an intimate small restaurant located just outside of Fonthill at the corner of Rice Road and Highway 20. The cosy forty-eight seat dining room is surrounded by large bay windows filled with plants, homegrown herbs, and greenery. Dried wildflowers hang from the wooden rafters creating a warm and inviting atmosphere.

Because the Wildflower is located in the heart of the Niagara region, Chef Wolfgang Sterr uses locally sourced products wherever possible. The menu consists of a variety of exquisitely presented dishes, including fresh seafood, lamb, beef, and vegetarian dishes. All sauces, dressings, and desserts are homemade. Niagara regional wines (VQA) are offered to complement the Wildflower's menu.

200 Highway 20 East
Fonthill, ON
L0S 1E6

Telephone: (905) 892-6167
Fax: (905) 892-4650

Open year-round
Lunch and dinner: Tuesday to Saturday
Sunday, bunch only
Seasonal: April to October, Sunday dinner
Reservations recommended
Restaurateurs: Wolfgang Sterr and Emily Schild

THE WILDWOOD INN RESTAURANT 44

The Wildwood Inn Restaurant is situated on the outskirts of the town of St. Marys, in the heart of the Perth County countryside. It is close to the Stratford Festival theatres and therefore hosts an international clientele.

The menu offers modern and traditional dishes, changing daily and featuring local organic produce. The dining room has a warm, casual ambiance, and the service is attentive and professional, hosted by Mary Woolf, the wife of chef Chris Woolf. The wine list is chosen from regular tastings and features Canadian and international wines and beers.

R.R. # 2
St. Marys, ON
N4X 1C5
Telephone: (519) 349-2467

Open February 14 through December 31
February 14 through May 31
Dinner: Friday and Saturday
June 1 through September 30
Breakfast, Lunch and Dinner: Tuesday through Saturday
October 1 through December 31
Dinner: Friday and Saturday
Restaurateurs: Chris and Mary Woolf

INDEX